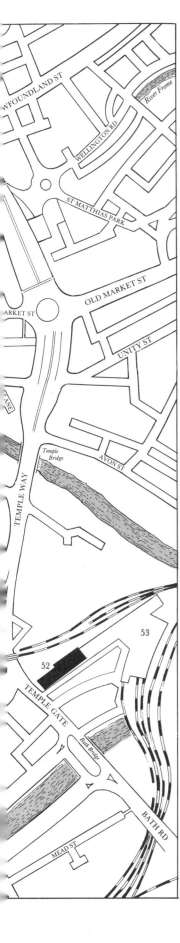

CENTRAL BRIS

CW00741801

KEY

1 Bristol Grammar School
2 University Refectory
3 City Museum and Art Gallery
4 Wills Memorial Building
5 Royal Fort House
6 Rupert's Gate
7 Bengough's Almshouses
8 Colston's Almshouses
9 St Michael's Church
10 Bristol Royal Infirmary
11 St James' Church
12 Broadmead Baptist Church
13 The New Room (John Wesley's Chapel)
14 Merchant Taylors' Almshouses
15 Quakers' Friars
16 The Red Lodge
17 Foster's Almshouses and the Chapel of the Three Kings
18 St Bartholomew's Hospital
19 Colston Hall
20 St Mary on the Quay
21 St Stephen's Church
22 Guildhall
23 St John's Gateway
24 Christ Church
25 All Saints Church
26 Corn Exchange
27 St Nicholas' Markets
28 St Nicholas' Church Museum
29 St Mary-le-Port

30 St Peter's Church
31 Church of St George
32 Georgian House Museum
33 Council House
34 Lord Mayor's Chapel (St Mark's)
35 Harveys Wine Museum
36 Central Library
37 Abbey Gateway
38 Bristol Cathedral
39 Cathedral School
40 Watershed Media Centre
41 Bristol Exhibition Centre
42 TSMV *Lochiel* (Inn on the Quay)
43 Arnolfini
44 Merchant Venturers' Almshouses
45 Theatre Royal
46 St Nicholas' Almshouses
47 Temple Church
48 Fairbairn Steam Crane
49 Bristol Industrial Museum and National Lifeboat Museum
50 St Mary Redcliffe
51 Fry's House of Mercy
52 Bristol Old Station
53 Temple Meads Station

▧ Pedestrianised areas

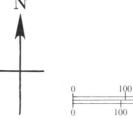

N

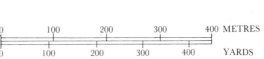

BRISTOL

TOWER LANE

BRISTOL

Text by
PAUL NEWMAN

With photographs by
ERNEST FRANKL

THE PEVENSEY PRESS
Cambridge England

Published by The Pevensey Press
6 De Freville Avenue, Cambridge CB4 1HR, UK

Acknowledgements
Photographs: Ernest Frankl. Permission to reproduce the following
photographs is gratefully acknowledged: **3, 24**: the City of Bristol;
16: Royal Fort House, University of Bristol; **18, 21**: The Very Revd
A. H. Dammers, Dean of Bristol; **25**: Harveys Wine Museum;
30: City of Bristol Museum and Art Gallery; **38**: Arnolfini Gallery;
40: Theatre Royal; **43, 44, 45**: the Vicar and Churchwarden of
St Mary Redcliffe; **53, 54**: The Revd Edwin A. Morris, Rector of the
City of Bristol; **60**: The New Room.

Maps: Carmen Frankl

Edited by Julia Harding

Designed by Kate Hughes-Stanton

Design and production in association with
Book Production Consultants, Cambridge

© Ernest Frankl and the Pevensey Press, 1987
First published 1987

ISBN 0 907115 35 7   hard covers
     0 907115 36 5   paperback

Origination by Anglia Graphics
Typesetting in Baskerville by Cambridge Photosetting Services
Printed and bound in Spain by Graficromo

Front cover The Cabot Tower, Brandon Hill

Frontispiece (**1**) St John's Gateway, the sole survivor of the medieval
entrances to the city

Back cover The stern of the SS *Great Britain*

Contents

Introduction

Bristol means 'bridging-point', and was originally used of the site where the Saxon fort and then the Norman castle stood; but the image of a bridge is, I think, still highly pertinent to this great city and its character. As a boy I went to school in Bristol, and I always remember that part of the bus journey when, on the approach to the Cumberland Basin, the Avon Gorge loomed up starkly with the immense castle-like warehouses squaring up in the foreground. The gaunt limestone cliffs, rifted and scarred with age, were vibrant with clinging greenery, and the Clifton Suspension Bridge (**2, 68**) – an elastic leap of cabled metal – brought to the scene a note of civilised triumph. The image of that

bridge, rather than the older Bristol Bridge, has become synonymous with the city. A bridge is an effort of connection. It spans gaps and quickens access, and that is what Bristol has achieved throughout its history. Its prosperity was always based upon establishing links – with Iceland, Europe and the New World – and this process continues today. Concorde, the most striking 20th-century symbol of the crossing of cultures and continents, was partly developed at Filton. Modern Bristol is an exciting melting-pot of the old and new, against a background of scenery varying from breezy downland to crowded dockland to sedate Georgian crescents.

1. History

PREVIOUS PAGE
*2 Isambard Kingdom
Brunel's masterpiece, the
Clifton Suspension
Bridge, spans the 250-
foot chasm of the Avon
Gorge, 245 feet above the
high water mark, between
Clifton and Leigh
Woods. It was opened in
December 1863, four
years after Brunel's
death.*

*3 The Lord Mayor's
Chapel, partly 13th
century, faces College
Green and is now
hemmed in by the more
modern buildings and
shops at the southern end
of Park Street, which
obscure the late-15th-
century tower. The
imposing west window,
also 15th century,
surmounts the entrance to
a treasure house of
beauty.*

There are remains of prehistoric encampments at such places as Stokeleigh, Clifton and Burgh Walls, but the port of Bristol became properly established in Saxon times. An elongated hillock engirdled by the curves of the Rivers Avon and Frome was the magnet for settlement, providing both safety and ready transport by water. The Saxons developed this into a fort, and Bricgstow, the 'settlement by the bridge', was recognised as a secure anchorage and trading post. From this modest complex a small port arose which rapidly expanded, and a mint opened under King Cnut (1017–35). Anglo-Saxon and Anglo-Norman coins minted in Bristol have been found as far away as Scandinavia, most likely part of the Danegeld exacted from England.

The Saxon town centred around the area of the modern Castle Park. When the Normans came, they were quick to annexe this strategic site. Geoffrey, Bishop of Coutances, one of the chief architects of the Domesday Survey, instigated the building of the motte and bailey in the late 11th century; Robert, Earl of Gloucester (who founded St James' priory church, see p. 77), added the huge keep of Caen stone; and the castle grew to be twice the size of Caernarvon. It was the residence of Queen Matilda, who kidnapped her royal cousin Stephen, and imprisoned him within its walls. Prince Henry (afterwards Henry II) was placed here for 'safety and education' for four years. Oliver Cromwell eventually razed the building during the Civil War, after it had served by turns as a Royalist and Parliamentarian stronghold, and only lately has the City Council restored its outline.

The Normans introduced a more stringent rule. Bristol did not have an unblemished reputation at this early period, and aroused the scorn and indignation of Bishop Wulfstan, who heavily criticised the town for its slave trade. Young boys and girls were shipped over to the Viking port of Dublin and exchanged for goods and money – a practice that may have been tempered by the Conqueror's interference.

By 1373 Bristol had been made a county, with its first acting sheriff or officer of the Crown. Although city status was not conferred until the middle of the 16th century, expansion was rapid. Another settlement had formed beyond the town walls, around the nucleus of Broad Street, Corn Street, Wine Street, Small Street and High Street. This medieval borough was itself enclosed by walls pierced by four main entrance gates, of which only St John's remains (see p. 72), adorned with the sculptures of the Gaulish chiefs Brennus and Belinus (**1**), fabled founders of the town (390 BC). The diversion of the River Frome in 1239 by the cutting of a new channel had transformed the dock complex, allowing for more quays and loading bays. Proximity to

Cotswold wool, together with availability of durable building stone and rich agricultural land, provided the incentive for foreign trade. The charter of 1373 demonstrates how the town's boundaries had extended to embrace such districts as St Augustine, St Michael, St James, SS Philip and Jacob, and Redcliffe, as well as the waters of the Avon and Severn as far as the islands of Steep Holm and Flat Holm.

The 15th century ushered in a further period of growth as merchants found outlets in Ireland, France, Holland and Spain. Cloth was the major export and wine the major import: wharves and cellars were piled high with bales and hogsheads. Gradually a new class of prosperous merchants and craftsmen emerged. They banded together to form guilds – akin to early trade unions – that laid down rules of practice and codes of behaviour. As they grew richer and increasingly influential the guilds became the moving force in the town. This development provoked concern when the sums amassed by certain wealthy traders rivalled, and sometimes exceeded, those of the established nobility. Henry VII fined Bristol's merchants 'because their wives so finely dressed' and flouted the sumptuary laws of the period. But their expenditure was not restricted to fine apparel. The guilds funded schools, churches, almshouses (**6**), hospitals and charities; individual benefactors subsidised the creation of splendid churches, the most outstanding being St Mary Redcliffe, which Queen Elizabeth I so admired. William Canynges put most of his fortune into this venture and eventually entered the priesthood himself, singing his first mass in 1468, an event still commemorated by the Rush Sunday service each Whitsuntide (see p. 56).

The medieval town was a place of great fairs; the most famous, on the

4 *A group of plaques at the head of St Augustine's Reach, beside the statue of Neptune (**34**), commemorates explorers who set sail from Bristol on voyages of discovery.*

5 *Tall Ships like this one are frequent visitors to Bristol Harbour.*

OVERLEAF
6 *The Merchant Venturers' Almshouses (1696–9) in King Street, originally established and funded by the guild as a home for retired seamen, as the verse on the wall indicates.*

festival of St James, took place at the Horsefair (now set squarely in the core of Broadmead shopping centre), and corn, skins, wool, fish and meat were traded. Foreign produce included oil, fruit and wine from Spain, spices from Alexandria, silks and glass from Venice. A throng of jugglers, jokers, ballad-mongers, dancers and tumblers provided moments of light relief.

Bristol traded with Iceland for fish but the course of the partnership seldom ran smooth. Nevertheless, it was probably through this remote volcanic island that merchants first heard of a fabulous land beyond the western seas which they called Brasylle. Maybe a residue of ancient Viking blood was stirred by the legend, for it seemed to stimulate fresh zeal for exploration. Men like John Cabot, Martin Pring, John Guy and Thomas James undertook ambitious voyages which culminated in the colonisation of the New World (4). John Cabot, who settled in Bristol in about 1495, was probably the most famous of these venturers. He set sail from Bristol in his tiny ship *Matthew*; on 14 June 1497 he caught sight of the mainland of North America, and disembarked there, hoisting the English banner and the Venetian flag. He returned to Bristol believing he had found the mainland of Cathay, and was awarded a pension of £20 a year by Henry VII. A personal cult arose around him, prompting an Italian observer to comment, 'Vast honour is paid to him, he dresses in silk, and the English run after him like mad people.'

Richard Hakluyt (1552–1616), a prebendary of Bristol, was one of the earliest historians of seagoing exploits, and inspired the creation of the first English colony in America. An age of resettlement began. During the 17th

11

Freed from all storms the tempest and the rage
Of billows here we spend our age
Our weather beaten vessels here repair
And from the Merchants kind and generous care
Find harbour here, no more we put to sea
Until we launch into Eternity.
And lest our Widows whom we leave behind
Should want relief they too a shelter find
Thus all our anxious cares and sorrows cease
Whilst our kind Guardians turn our toils to ease
May they be with an endless Sabbath blest
Who have afforded unto us this rest

century ships sailed from Bristol laden with families and single men of all types and classes, including refugees from religious persecution, nobility displaced by the Civil War, fortune hunters and those intent on finding a new life in a virgin land. As a result, trade between Britain and the New World increased. Tobacco from Barbados and Virginia was imported through Bristol and the smoking habit became so widespread among both women and men that Monsieur de Rochefort, Treasurer of France, commented that many 'think that without Tobacco one cannot live in England because they say it dissipates the humours of the brain'. Another commodity was sugar from the West Indies, and, on a visit to Bristol in 1654, John Evelyn the diarist noted how it was refined and formed into loaves; he enjoyed 'a collation of eggs fried in the sugar furnace with excellent Spanish wine'.

Increased consumption of these products required increased productivity; demand for labour grew until England found the answer in African slaves, who could be bought cheaply with such items as trinkets, firearms and hardware and then shipped to the West Indies, where they were worked until they expired. In 1725 some 16,550 slaves were carried to plantations by Bristol ships and it is sometimes alleged that only half that number survived the voyages. The slave ships, called 'Blackbirds', aroused the ire of such men as William Wilberforce; and, in a letter to the reformer, John Wesley referred to the trade as 'that execrable villainy which is the scandal of religion, of England and of human nature'.

Religious dissent has a prominent role in the history of Bristol, which seems to have been relatively hospitable to the different Nonconformist sects. The early Quakers John Audland and Thomas Airey visited the city in 1654 and preached to the Baptists, whose Broadmead church survives today. William Penn, founder of Pennsylvania, was a leading Bristol Quaker and the house of the Dominican Friars (now called the Quakers' Friars; **7**), bought in 1760, remained the chief meeting place of the Society of Friends for some three hundred years.

The Quakers' religious initiative was followed by the grass-roots evangelising of the Methodists. After his return from America, George Whitefield turned his attention to Bristol and particularly to the industrial population, including the Kingswood miners, who had little contact with education or religion. In 1739 he was joined by John Wesley. Their fire and ardour soon stirred hostility and they were barred from most parish churches. For a time they were forced to preach in the open air, as they had done in Georgia, but eventually Wesley acquired land in the Horsefair and erected the New Room, the first Methodist chapel in the world (**60**).

Prosperity in the 18th century nurtured an architectural style of cool aplomb, epitomised in Clifton village, which is still a distinct area famous for its Georgian and Regency squares, crescents and terraces. While such elegant edifices arose amidst the meadows and greenery, businessmen were establishing what were to become major companies. Joseph Fry, a Quaker, started his chocolate factory in 1761; the Wills family began selling tobacco and snuff in 1786. Meanwhile the time-honoured trades of glassmaking, pottery and porcelain continued to flourish. On the bustling quays of the city barrels of rum and bales of tobacco were constantly being unloaded and taken away on horse-drawn sledges. One of the visitors drawn to this animated scene, the poet Alexander Pope, described in a letter dated 1739 the hundreds of ships,

7 *Part of Quakers' Friars, formerly the cloisters of a 13th-century Dominican friary: an oasis of tranquillity within the bustling Broadmead shopping centre.*

'their Masts as thick as they can stand by one another', sprouting dramatically among the tight-packed grubby dwellings and narrow dark streets.

The death-throes of the Regency period were marked by rioting and reform. Franchise was the issue of the day. Charles Wetherell, Recorder of Bristol, opposed the Reform Bill, stating that the fever for change had abated in Bristol. This crass assertion aroused the anger of the mob, who resisted the troops sent in to quell them. Wetherell himself, a man who was by turns eccentric, ribald and preposterous, escaped from the city by climbing over the outbuildings in disguise. The rioters, now drunk, began firing the gaols, toll houses, public buildings and various citadels of the rich. A letter of 1831 by Mrs William Fedden brings home something of the reality of the Bristol Riots:

> Directly opposite, and as you know, but a short distance from us was Bridewell, likewise in flames; then came Queen Square, which I must fail in attempting to describe, the flames towering to the skies, and the long volume of smoke which the wind blew this way, curling in a thousand varied forms; now and then balls of fire would be blown into the air and carried to a considerable distance, while the reflection of the light on the surrounding trees, various steeples and distant landscape formed a scene terrific indeed, but at the same time beautifully awful.

15

8 *Isambard Kingdom Brunel, designer and engineer of genius, presiding over the traffic on Broad Quay.*

About six hundred people died; the west and north sides of Queen Square, including the Customs House and the Mansion House, were burnt, as was the Bishop's Palace, next to the cathedral.

The reign of Victoria brought railways, canals, Macadamised roads and spectacular enterprises in civil engineering, exemplified by the achievements of Isambard Kingdom Brunel (1806–59; **8**). He had come to Clifton to convalesce after a debilitating illness, and quickly established himself as a technological innovator. Not only did he win the Clifton bridge competition (see p. 90) but he also went on to plan the Great Western Railway, linking London to Bristol, and to design the *Great Britain* steamship (**48**). Temple Meads Station (see pp. 79–80) stands as a monument to his functional artistry. Mary Russell Mitford, a poet and novelist who visited Clifton in 1843, bore witness to Brunel's growing prestige and reported enthusiastically on the city:

> Of Bath, its buildings and scenery, I had heard much good; of Bristol, its dirt and its dinginess, its ugliness, much evil. Shall I confess – dare I confess – that I was charmed with the old city? . . .
>
> The tall picturesque dwellings with their quaint gables, the wooden houses in Wine Street, one of which was brought from Holland bodily [the Dutch House, destroyed during the blitz] . . . the courts and lanes climbing like ladders up the steep aclivities, the hanging gardens, said to have been given by Queen Elizabeth to the washerwomen (everything has a tradition in Bristol), the bustling quays, the crowded docks, the calm, silent Dowry Parade with its trees growing up between the pavement like the close of a cathedral.
>
> The Avon flowing between those two exquisite boundaries – the richly tufted Leigh Woods clothing the steep hillside and the grand and lofty St Vincent's Rocks with houses perched upon the summits that looked ready to fall upon our heads; the airy line of the chain that swung from tower to tower of the intended Suspension Bridge with its basket hanging in mid-air like the car of a balloon making one dizzy to look at it, formed an enchanting picture.

The 20th century inaugurated a series of cultural and scientific innovations, beginning with the Art Gallery, opened in 1905. Six years later the aeroplane factory was operating at Filton and 1925 saw the completion of the new University Building (see p. 42). The following year the Portway route was laid between Bristol and Avonmouth. The Second World War wreaked destruction at the heart of the city but the ensuing peace saw a determined recovery. A spectacular, relatively recent event was the birth of Concorde (1970), which truly set the tone for the second half of this century. Aerospace now figures among Bristol's major industries, with food, drink, tobacco, printing, packaging, chemicals, paints, plastics and the ubiquitous microchip. Since the end of the 1960s there has been a concerted effort to restore buildings of special historical and architectural interest, and a major conservation programme has created a renaissance in the heart of Bristol. The city cherishes its heritage and keeps abreast of the times, blending tradition and technology, pageantry and progressiveness.

2. The Centre and St Michael's Hill

The area known as the Centre lies just outside the medieval town wall, whose line is traced by Colston Avenue and Quay Street. It has a lively variety of architecture, from looming towers of plate glass to ancient timbered foundations such as St Bartholomew's Hospital. Vibrant with brashness and bustle, it is an intensely exhilarating centre, relieved by water, greenery, broken skylines and fascinating statuary.

The figure of Edward Colston (1636–1721; **9**) stands on a paved traffic island opposite the Church of St Mary on the Quay. Twisty-tailed dolphins disport themselves around the base and several plaques illustrate the benefactor's charitable deeds. Unveiled in 1895, it was the work of the Manchester sculptor John Cassidy, and depicts Colston as an old man, 'one of the most virtuous and wise sons of the city', looking pensive yet commanding, a long cane propping up his right elbow. A ubiquitous personage in Bristol, he founded almshouses and two schools, and gave over £70,000 to his native city. Yet he was also involved in the slave trade, and stipulated that only children of Anglicans should attend his schools: like many other fundamentally generous men, he was convention-bound and had a narrow range of emotional sympathies. A temperamental contrast to Colston was the Anglo-Irish politician and philosopher Edmund Burke (**10**), now similarly exposed to the hurly-burly of the city centre. Unveiled in 1894 by Lord Rosebery, he stands on a pedestal of pink granite and is a replica of a marble statue in the House of Commons carved by the younger William Theed. Burke was elected to represent Bristol in 1774. Opposed to the government's anti-American policies which threatened trade, he gained favour locally, but subsequently forfeited it by being too much his own man. He lost his Parliamentary seat in 1780 because he supported proposals to relax restrictions on trade between Ireland and Britain, and to alleviate laws against Catholics.

The tower and Corinthian portico of St Mary on the Quay can be clearly identified from here. Designed by R. S. Pope for the Catholic Apostolic, or Irvingite, faction, it was soon acquired by the Roman Catholics and opened in 1843. At present it is used by the priests of the Society of Jesus. Its name revives memories of times when ships seemed to be moored in the very streets, before the Frome was filled in and diverted.

St Augustine's Parade is the name given to the fine group of buildings – showing a vivid mix of Tudor and Flemish gables – that used to overlook the River Frome. The old Tramways Clock stands out prominently, a reminder that this was once a tram-lined area: St Augustine's Back (the old name for the stretch of water that flowed here) became the Tramways Centre in 1875 when the first line was laid.

9, 10 Though they were worlds apart in political opinion and style, Edward Colston and James Burke now stand within about a hundred yards of one another, in the middle of the Centre.

18

OVERLEAF
11 *Christmas Steps, usually thronged with people but seen here in the early morning, were cut in 1669 to improve the steep route down to the bank of the River Frome.*

12 *At the bottom of Christmas Steps, almost hidden beside the 17th-century timber-framed fish and chip shop, is the medieval entrance arch of St Bartholomew's, precious remnant of the 13th-century hospital.*

The Hippodrome (1900), which forms part of St Augustine's Parade, has the largest provincial stage in Britain and a seating capacity of 2,000. The London Contemporary Dance Theatre gives regular performances here, as do the Welsh Opera Company and many other internationally famous touring groups. The dark crimson interior has true Edwardian panache: Art Nouveau lettering, giant fluted Roman Doric columns, and naked caryatids.

An even larger venue for popular entertainment is the nearby Colston Hall, in Colston Street. The building (1867–73) was designed by Foster and Wood and has a decorous Italianate façade in yellow brick and terracotta. Fires have destroyed the interior twice, but it has been thoughtfully restored and modernised. The four-manual organ has a mobile console and is a most versatile instrument. The Beatles, Rolling Stones, Syd Lawrence, Little Richard, Frank Sinatra – all luminaries of light entertainment – have appeared here.

By contrast, the porter's lodge of St Bartholomew's Hospital, at the bottom of Christmas Steps, plunges the visitor deep into the vaults of history. Timber-framing adds atmosphere to this ancient archway (**12**), which led to the courtyard of the hospital, founded before 1207 for elderly sailors but now obliterated. Subsequently Bristol Grammar School (1532) and Queen Elizabeth's Hospital (1766) annexed the building. The archway, restored in 1984, is decorated with a mutilated statue of the Virgin in a style that recalls the façade at Wells Cathedral.

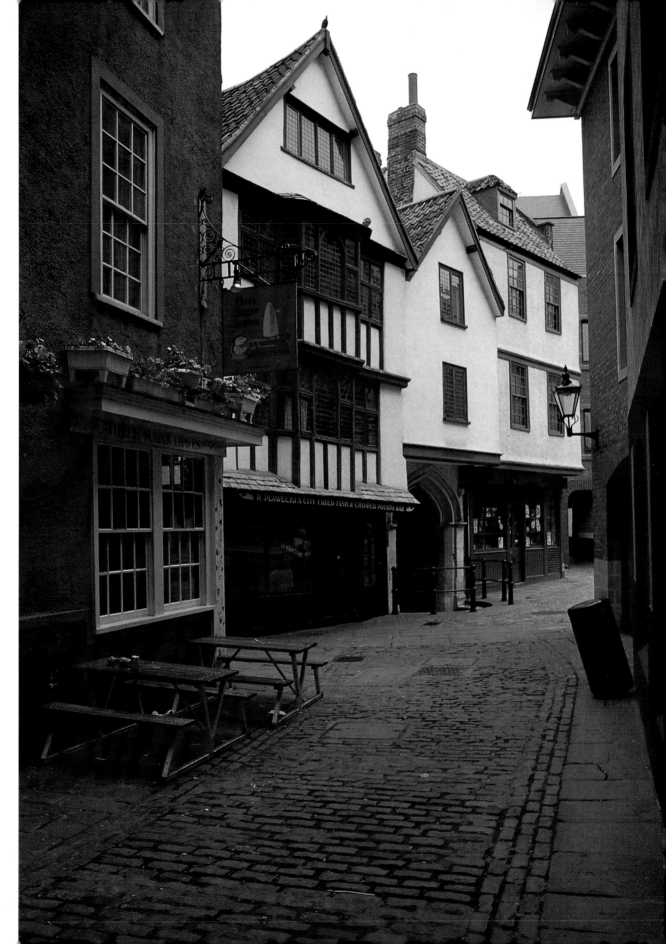

Christmas Steps (**11**), intriguing, colourful and pigeon-haunted, were originally a steep short-cut linking the northern back of the River Frome with what is now Colston Street. Today they look almost chic, having lost something of their old murky ambience. There are tidy Georgian shops dealing in prints, stamps, gold and jewellery, and hand-made shoes. The steps were cut by Jonathan Blackwell, a wealthy wine merchant and later Alderman of London, who also provided lanterns with seats on either side for tired wayfarers. These were replaced during the 19th century by the gas lamps which now line the centre of the alley. Its crammed, shadowy, jumbled quality makes it a most Dickensian nook, though it has lost its marvellously cluttered bookshop, laden with the mustiest, dustiest tomes, that featured in an early Cliff Richard film.

Opposite the top of Christmas Steps, the magic and joke shop presents a suitably hilarious display of masks, fright wigs and various comic bits of the human anatomy. Of more interest to antiquarians is the Chapel of the Three Kings (**13**), and the adjoining Foster's Almshouses. These buildings were initially funded in 1483–4 by the wealthy salt merchant John Foster, who served successively as Bailiff, Sheriff, and Mayor of Bristol, becoming the town's Member of Parliament in 1489. He had visited the Continent, and probably the city of Cologne, where, in the cathedral treasury, he could have seen the gold shrine holding the relics of the three kings: Melchior, King of Nubia and Arabia, who offered gold to the infant Christ; Kaspar, King of Tarsus and Egypt, who offered frankincense; and Balthazar, who hailed from Godolia and Saba, and presented his gift of myrrh. Over the door of Foster's Chapel are the traceried niches for the statues of the three kings (now filled with modern replacements by the Bristol sculptor Ernest Pascoe, contributed in 1967).

The almshouses consisted of 14 rooms to accommodate eight poor men and four or five poor women, together with a priest, who was to receive £4 a year. The inmates were provided with pocket money of 2d a week, guaranteed to them for forty years, also with small gardens to grow vegetables and herbs. The present almshouses date from 1861 and are the design of John Foster (no relation), who favoured a busily ornate Burgundian domestic Gothic, with gables, porches, crocketed finials and spired turrets.

From the top of Christmas Steps, Lower Park Row ascends to Park Row itself. After the visual diversity and splendour of Park Street (see Ch. 4), this area seems almost a shabby, neglected backwater, the road sweeping down past the Royal Infirmary (founded 1735) and the prosaic bus station. But it has its hidden secrets, the best of which is The Red Lodge (**14**), a rebuilt Elizabethan lodge house on the corner of Park Row and Lodge Street. It was one of two in the grounds of the Great House, erected by Sir John Young in 1590 on the site now occupied by the Colston Hall. Queen Elizabeth I stayed at the Great House and later it was the home of Robert Yate, Mayor and Member of Parliament for Bristol. Externally The Red Lodge is orthodox Georgian, with tidy regular windows and modillioned cornice, but inside, on the first floor, is the last surviving suite of 16th-century rooms in Bristol, splendidly preserved. The panelling and carved-stone chimneypiece in the Great Oak Room are especially magnificent.

The lodge was a girl's reformatory from 1854 until 1919, founded and run by Mary Carpenter. She was assisted by Lady Byron, who, after her brief,

13 *The Chapel of the Three Kings, Colston Street: modern statues of the three kings by Ernest Pascoe (1967) in the early-16th-century niches on the south front.*

15 *The top of St Michael's Hill affords a good view over the city.*

15 *The top of St Michael's Hill affords a good view over the city.*

disastrous marriage to the poet, became interested in altering minds and morals. Mary Carpenter was left a stock of her correspondence, among which was the poet's farewell to his wife:

> Fare thee well and if forever
> Still, forever, fare thee well.

This noble valediction was written on the back of an unpaid butcher's bill.

St Michael's Hill (**15**) forks away to the left as one descends Perry Road, the eastern extension of Park Row. The hill and the local church take their name from the warrior saint and monarch of all high places. The church is often called St Michael's-on-the-Mount-Without, because it lies beyond the environs of the city. It has a fine 15th-century Perpendicular tower and a handsome Georgian interior (1775) by Thomas Paty. Notable as one climbs St Michael's Hill are the many desirable tall 17th- and 18th-century houses with smart colour-washed fronts and the broad, raised pavements on the left. Education has moved in here, and so has public health (there are several hospital and University buildings), but the best sight is perhaps the stuccoed walls, pedimented windows, neat slender chimneys and trim front lawns of Colston's Almshouses (1695; **17**). Colston erected them for twelve men and sixteen women, stipulating a preference for those who had lived in 'some sort of decency' rather than 'drunkards' or those 'of a vicious life', who would not make convivial neighbours.

These almshouses interestingly compare with the handsome Queen Anne group in Horfield Road, set over to the north-east, which was the gift of

14 *The Red Lodge (c. 1590) turns its back on the street and faces downhill, the generously transomed and mullioned windows overlooking a Tudor-style garden laid out in 1983.*

25

16 *Thomas Stocking was responsible for the exquisite stucco ceilings (c. 1760) in Royal Fort House, once the home of Thomas Tyndall and now the Music Department of the University of Bristol.*

Alderman Bengough to the Corporation. Bengough knew that he was dying in 1817 and proposed that deeds be drawn up to arrange an appropriate endowment. Accommodation was provided for fifteen single women and five single men or married couples, with a weekly allowance of 7s each. Bengough died shortly after and is commemorated by a monument in the Lord Mayor's Chapel (see p. 35), but the houses were not built until 1878; they are very elegant and substantial, with a central triangular pediment, railings and a formal stepped entrance.

Royal Fort Road (on the left as one climbs St Michael's Hill) leads into Tankard's Close. This once went by the name 'Stinkard's Close', holding grim memories of the plague which visited Bristol in 1645. Pitch and Pay Lane, joining Durdham Down and Stoke Bishop, acquired its name during this period. The villagers would not trade their wares in Bristol for fear of infection: thus they bargained with citizens from a safe distance, the food and merchandise being thrown over a stile. Tankard's Close, similarly, was a place for 'airing' those who came from the diseased areas. Despite such precautions, the infection took hold and there were many victims.

Rupert's Gate is at the end of the cul-de-sac branching off at the junction of Royal Fort Road and Tankard's Close. From this point, in 1643, during the Civil War, Prince Rupert swept down and took the city for the Royalists. He held it until 1645, when he ordered the burning of all of Clifton and part of

Westbury to impede the advancing Parliamentarians; but then Colonel Fairfax, Cromwell's second-in-command, besieged it and forced a surrender. The way by which Rupert left his fort coincided with the route to the public gallows – a busy thoroughfare, alive with the feet of the tramping mob.

Beyond Rupert's Gate stands Royal Fort House; part of the University since 1916, it accommodates the departments of music and theology. Not to be confused with the castle-like Physics Building standing opposite, it got its name from the fortress erected on this site by Prince Rupert in 1643. The architect James Bridges designed the house (c. 1760) for the merchant Thomas Tyndall, who obviously appreciated a good interior, for he employed Thomas Stocking to do the plasterwork, which is superb (**16**). Vines ascend the walls of the staircase hall with sinuous delicacy and swags of fruit and founts of foliage leaf among the archways, while the beautiful stucco on the ceilings of the dining and withdrawing rooms and the parlour justifies Stocking's international reputation. A poem celebrating Tyndall's enterprise, probably by John Wallis, was published in *Felix Farley's Bristol Journal* in 1767:

17 *Set back from St Michael's Hill, these neat and well-kept almshouses were founded by Edward Colston in 1695.*

> Long in neglect, an ancient Dwelling stood
> 　With tottering Walls, worn Roofs, and perish'd Wood,
> Till gen'rous Tyndal, fir'd with Sense and Taste
> 　Saw here confusion, – Ruin there, – and Waste
> Resolved at once to take the Rubbish down,
> And raise a Palace there to grace the TOWN. . .

3. Bristol Cathedral and College Green

Bristol Cathedral is a building of great power, simplicity and decorum, retaining the original Norman chapter house and many other remnants of its foundation. In 1140, Robert Fitzharding, Provost of Bristol and ancestor of the Earls of Berkeley, founded an Augustinian abbey on the hillside overlooking the walled medieval town. The abbey church, probably consecrated in 1165, now stands as the supreme achievement of Edmund Knowle, abbot 1306–32, who 'bilded the churche of the new fro the Fundamentes w^t the vestrary . . . He bilde also of the new from the Fundamentes the Kynges Hall. And also the Kynges Chamber. Also he reparid. And kevered the Freytoure w^t othir goode dedis.' Knowle's rebuilding of the eastern end of the church and the choir moved Nikolaus Pevsner to write: 'It proves incontrovertibly that English design surpassed that of all other countries during the first third of the c14.'

Like many other abbey churches, it had its periods of moral laxity, when professional piety proved a strain and the diversions of the secular world too strong to resist. In 1278 Bishop Godfrey Giffard, on a tour of inspection, admonished the canons. The accounts were suspect, and the granary-keeper, the corn-seller and the porter were dismissed. The canons were warned not to meet in the infirmary 'for the sake of drinking and surfeiting' and were forbidden to indulge in 'detraction and obscene speech'. They were also ordered 'not as bees to fly out of the Choir as soon as the Service was ended, as vagrants and vagabonds, but devoutly to wait as became holy and settled persons'.

At the Court of Chancery (1540), Nicholas Corbet, priest of St Philip's, Bristol, testified 'that when they were Canons dwelling in the monastery of St Augustine's, Bristol, now dissolved, he knew John Rastle to be a great dicer and carder, and had heard that he had got at dice and cards of divers men in his chamber at the late monastery £10, £5 and 5 marks, especially the year before the dissolution of the monastery'.

In 1590 Dr Richard Fletcher was appointed to the see of Bristol (it had become a diocese in 1542) and the Corporation welcomed him with a gift of 30 gallons of sack and 20 pounds of sugar. He was the father of the dramatist John Fletcher and drew a rebuke from Queen Elizabeth for 'cutting his beard too short'. Tobacco is thought to have been his downfall, for he died in 1596, still smoking heavily, 'with his fayre lady and her carpets and cushions in her bedchamber'.

During the Bristol Riots (1831), the cathedral suffered great damage: the Bishop's Palace was burnt down; a fire was lit in the chapter house; valuable

18 *The High Altar and carved stone reredos in Bristol Cathedral were rebuilt by John Pearson in 1899, after the completion of the new nave.*

books and documents were destroyed; and it was left to Gilbert Scott to re-embellish and restore (c. 1860) at a cost of £12,000.

The awe-inspiring nave was planned by Abbot Newland (1481–1515) to replace the Norman one. He built the outer walls on the north side and west end to the level of the sills of the windows, but the work was abandoned after the Dissolution, demolished and built over. It was not until 1868 that G. E. Street was commissioned to rebuild the nave and west end. He closely followed the old plan, 'intending to harmonize without slavish copying of the details'; the result is the only English hall-church – where the roofs of aisles and nave go up to the same height – to a medieval design. Shafts of blue lias vary the preponderance of Corsham stone used in the clustering columns and the effect is both spacious and imposing.

As one moves from the nave into the choir (**18**), it is noticeable that whereas the nave vault-ribs join a central ridge, those of the choir form kite-shaped compartments, foliated and cusped. This distinctive and beautiful lierne-vaulting, as it is called, was the work of Abbot Knowle in the early 14th century. The unusual substitution of side-lighting for top or clerestory lighting in the choir and aisles successfully avoids the lighting defect apparent in many Norman churches. The arcades are soaring, lofty, with piers carrying triple shafts crowned by exuberant foliage capitals. But the most remarkable feature of the aisles is again the vaulting. The transoms serve as internal flying buttresses, studded with ball flowers and supporting fan-like vaulting ribs which rest on brackets of finely carved human heads.

The misericord carvings under the seats in the choir abound with virile energy. They depict the bucolic romps of the period: a man riding a sow, dancing bears, pig-killing and wrestling.

19 *The cathedral rises boldly on the southern side of College Green, a fine setting for summertime pagaentry.*

30

The Elder Lady Chapel lies north of the choir and aisles. The name distinguishes it from the Eastern Lady Chapel, also dedicated to the Virgin, but put up some fifty years later. The Elder Lady Chapel was begun by Abbot David soon after 1215. He hired some of the workmen from Wells, who were perhaps responsible for the most animated stone carvings. St Michael is shown dispatching the dragon-devil; a bird pecks at foliage; a monkey plays the bagpipes and a ram accompanies him on the violin; a goat carries a hare slung on a pole over his back – a banquet of pictorial humour. Here also is the tomb of Maurice, 9th Lord Berkeley (d. 1368), wearing a conical helmet and chain mail covered with plate. He was wounded and taken prisoner at Poitiers and ransomed for 6000 nobles (£2,000).

The Eastern Lady Chapel was begun in 1298. On its great early-14th-century reredos-screen are carved the leopards of England, the crosses of Berkeley and the chevrons of Clare (Maurice, Lord Berkeley, married a de Clare in 1316), and inside the arches the walls are adorned with gilded and coloured diaper work. The stellate wall niches contain statues of such abbots as Newbury (d. 1473), responsible for the central tower; Hunt (d. 1481), who vaulted the north transepts; and Newland, who rebuilt the gatehouse and refectory. The candlesticks on the altar date from 1712. They were presented to the cathedral by John Romsey, Town Clerk of Bristol, and are incised with two three-masted vessels, probably the *Duke* and *Duchess* – ships part-owned by Romsey that picked up castaway Alexander Selkirk (the original of Defoe's Robinson Crusoe) after his lonely vigil on the Juan Fernandez Islands.

20 *The peaceful cemetery garden of Bristol Cathedral, east of the chapter house.*

In the south transept is a sculptured coffin lid, perhaps Saxon, depicting the Harrowing of Hell (**21**), from a passage in the apocryphal book of Nicodemus, when, after the Crucifixion, Christ descended into the kingdom of fire and 'brought salvation to the souls held captive there'. The carving was found under the floor of the chapter house and is treasured for its mixture of energy and naivety. Christ is shown trampling down the denizens of Hell (one is falcon-headed like the god Horus) while rescuing a lost soul, who has been identified as Eve.

The chapter house adjoins the south transept. Before the Dissolution, it was used for such instructional purposes as the reading of the abbey rules, allocating work tasks, and the correction of breaches of discipline. The room is rectangular and has a variety of Norman decoration: zigzag mouldings, rich capitals and beaded cable string courses. The east wall and window are modern – the old ones were destroyed in the 1831 riots. The north and south walls are divided into three tiers: arcaded recesses which were used as seats by the monks, pillared arcades, and lattice moulding.

The cloisters date from the 15th century, yet there are earlier fragments such as the fine Norman arch on the south side of the cloister court, decorated with zigzag and interlace. Opposite the vestibule of the chapter house are two windows depicting the founders of the abbey and cathedral: St Augustine (probably apocryphal) and Abbots Newland and Elyot. The timbered roof is modern and so is the north walk, though the latter is decorated with old stonework and memorials to such men as Bird, the artist, and John Eagles, painter and poet. At the south end are other monuments, notably to Jane Porter (1776–1850), author of *The Scottish Chiefs*, and Harriet Hesketh (1733–1807), 'the merry and lovely cousin' of the poet Cowper. The deanery, close by, probably occupies the site of the King's Hall erected by Abbot Knowle and has fragments of Norman, Decorated and Perpendicular work.

The Bristol Cathedral School, which occupies the south range of the cloister, was refounded in 1542 by Henry VIII. The first grammar school had been attached to St Augustine's Abbey (1140), so the school is now over eight hundred years old.

The archway of the Abbey Gateway (west of the cathedral on Deanery Road) is remarkable for the dexterity and joyous mobility of its carving. Riband, zigzag and chevron mouldings succeed each other in a remarkable display of exuberant intricacy. The niches on the south side of the 16th-century upper storey, facing College Square, have four life-size figures in Portland Stone: above, Abbot Knowle (1306–32) holds a model of the church, and Abbot Snow (1332–41), the first mitred abbot, clutches a scroll; below them, Abbot Newland (1481–1515), the abbey chronicler, holds a book, and Abbot Elyot (1515–26) a model of the gateway.

The Central Library next door (1906, by Charles Holden) may owe something to the Glasgow modernist Charles Rennie Mackintosh, yet it expertly blends in with the Abbey Gateway. The architectural historian Bryan Little called it 'Jacobean Gothic', with its 'transomed ground floor . . . and somewhat fussy little oriels', but that does not quite convey the total impact. It uses Gothic lines and Tudor details, but simplifies and minimises them, so that the effect is restrained yet elaborate (**22**). The library is well equipped, with an excellent reference section on the city and local history.

The Council House (begun 1935, by Vincent Harris) was successfully

21 *One of the oldest relics in the cathedral, this vigorous carving of the Harrowing of Hell, possibly Saxon, was originally a coffin lid.*

designed so as not to clash with – or upset the harmony of – the cathedral. A calmly curving though suitably imperious façade with end-pavilions culminates in a central, domed porch enclosing the statue of an Elizabethan seaman (**23**). Gilded unicorns prance on the pavilions' sloping roofs – supporters of the city coat of arms. A strip of water, animated by gushing fountains, enhances the approach and adds lustre to the pigeon-pecked greensward, trembling lime trees, old houses and clean-lined modern shops. This is a place to relax on a sunny day, magnificent yet highly amenable, and inviting benches provide the opportunity.

The interior contains imposing relics and ceremonial decor. The main hall is paved in Belgian black marble and Bianco del Mar. Here is a blue and gold clock encircled by the signs of the zodiac and incorporating a wind indicator, and here also are paintings of the seven Royal Navy ships which have been called HMS *Bristol*. The Conference Hall has a pale abstract ceiling painted in egg tempera on a gesso ground by Tom Monnington – it is one of the largest painted ceilings in the country. The Council Chamber, fitted out with press and public galleries, is furnished in black-veneered oak and upholstered in crimson. The canvas on the ceiling, by John Armstrong, depicts 'Bristol at all times in its history' and includes merchant ships, modern airliners and figures representing Wisdom, Enterprise, Navigation and Industry. English walnut provides an opulent and comfortable feel to the Committee Rooms, and the Lord Mayor's Parlour displays the civic swords, which date from the 14th to the 18th century, as well as eight silver maces and two silver trumpets. The city archives are here as well, in air-conditioned strongrooms, and include rare books, notably Ricart's Kalendar (1479), a continuing calendar history of each mayor's year of office.

22 *The eclectic Central Library (1906), on Deanery Road next to the Abbey Gateway; a remarkable early work by Charles Holden, who later went on to design Underground stations in London.*

23 *The Council House, College Green, begun in 1935 and completed after the Second World War, during which Bristol suffered heavily from bombing raids.*

Across College Green, inconspicuous from outside, is the Lord Mayor's Chapel, dedicated to St Mark (**3**). Today the property of the Corporation, it is also the single remnant of the medieval Hospital of the Gaunts, founded in 1220 by Sir Maurice de Gaunt and his nephew Robert de Gournay. Having served as a church for the hospital, it was bought by the city in 1541 after the Dissolution. The interior is very interesting and should not be missed. Among its treasures are early French and English stained glass (**24**); the exquisite chantry chapel of the Roman Catholic Poyntz family (founded by Sir Robert Poyntz who died in 1520), fan-vaulted and set with Spanish tiles; and the virile iron-work of William Edney.

Above a shop in College Green, a short way south of the chapel, Langford's electric clock catches the eye. This was one of the earliest timepieces to indicate Greenwich Mean Time rather than Bristol Time (some two minutes difference), reflecting the need for synchronisation as communication between the ports strengthened. Harveys Wine Museum, in Denmark Street behind the chapel, incorporates the 13th-century cellars of Gaunts' Hospital. The dominance of the House of Anjou in the 12th century gave rise to the Bristol wine trade. When Henry II married Eleanor of Aquitaine, England acquired many of the finest wine-growing districts in France. This connection formed the bedrock of the success of later firms, including Harveys (established 1796), today renowned for its Bristol Milk, Bristol Cream, and other types of sherry. The Wine Museum (open to the public on Friday mornings) has an

25 *Part of the fascinating collection on display in Harveys Wine Museum.*

extensive collection of 18th-century drinking glasses, plus antique corkscrews, decanters, bottles and labels – in fact, everything an intoxicologist could wish for (**25**).

Opposite the northern end of Denmark Street stands The Hatchete, a pub which has associations with such pugilists as Tom Cribb (1781–1848), immortalised in verse by Lord Byron, and was also a centre of cock-fighting. The brash new Entertainments Centre in Frogmore Street overshadows it, providing a good venue for ice-skating and cinema-going, quite unlike the dignified Georgian façades with elegant entrances and footscrapers that grace nearby Orchard Street (1717).

24 *St Mark's, the Lord Mayor's Chapel since 1731, is crammed with works of great beauty. This eastern end of the chancel was given by Bishop Miles Salley (d. 1516). The early-16th-century stained glass is thought to have come from France.*

4. Park Street, Brandon Hill and Queen's Road

Park Street is Bristol's major thoroughfare. The Gothic coronet of the Wills Memorial Building (commonly known as the University Tower) provides a dramatic climax to the ascending line of shop-fronts and surging traffic. The bookstores, restaurants and wine-bars of this elegant, yet boisterously active, street admirably convey the brighter feel of the city. Near the foot of the incline, on the left as one ascends, stands the Masonic Hall (1823), designed by C. R. Cockerell. A frieze over the doorway shows Apollo and Minerva, two of the most cultivated inhabitants of Olympus, educating the city in the arts and sciences. This is not an esoteric Masonic code, but a reminder that the

27 *Charlotte Street from Brandon Hill.*

26 *The Wills Memorial Building (1925), known locally as the University Tower, dominates the southern end of Queen's Road. On the left is the University Refectory (1872), based on the Doge's Palace in Venice, and formerly the Bristol Museum; all but the façade was destroyed in the blitz. In the centre stands the present City Museum and Art Gallery (1899–1904), by Sir Frank Wills.*

building was originally a museum of natural science, antiquity and the arts.

The house on the corner of Park Street and Great George Street was the residence of Henry Cruger, born in New York State in 1739. Member of Parliament, Mayor of Bristol, and Master of the Merchant Venturers in 1781, he returned to New York in 1790, where he finished his distinguished career as a senator. The south-east side of Great George Street has a number of houses (c. 1790) by William Paty. A particularly fine example is No. 7, the home of the West India merchant John Pretor Pinney, now a museum known as The Georgian House. Three floors are on view, displaying among much else a gilded mirror, chandeliers, a superb cabinet (c. 1745) attributed to John Channon, and 18th-century views of Bristol. There is a tradition that Wordsworth and Coleridge first met here. Certainly Pinney was friendly with the poets, Wordsworth particularly, giving them occasional financial leg-ups in times of need. Life below stairs, all scrubbing, polishing and washing, is vividly evoked by the basement rooms. 'I now subscribe to a Cold Bath', Pinney wrote to a friend, 'and goes in every morning which I finds to be of great service to me.' This Arctic installation survives, 10 feet by 5 feet and cast in stone. Pinney must have been a man of great physical courage.

Across the street is the Church of St George (1823) by Robert Smirke, which is entered from Charlotte Street (**27**). Now used solely as a concert venue, this was the last church in the city to be built on classical lines, before the Gothic revival rendered the skyline spiky with spires, crockets and finials. William Friese-Green, the inventor of cinematography, was married here. The Greek Doric portico rests on four columns which surmount a long flight of steps, and there is a crowning cupola to sweeten the rather gauntly imposing composition. The acoustics of the building are excellent and Radio 3 regularly broadcasts live concerts from here.

Great George Street shelters under the towering slopes of Brandon Hill, which is 259 feet high and takes its name from St Brendan (484–577) who is said to have built a chapel on its summit. There was a hermitage or oratory near the top, which was once occupied by a female recluse, Lucy de Newchurch, who, in 1351, asked the Bishop of Worcester for permission to quit the world and shut herself up in the hermitage of St Brendan of Bristol. William of Worcester visited the chapel in the 15th century and recorded its dimensions – 27 feet by 16 feet. He asked the resident hermit the height of the chapel above the city and was told that the altitude of the cell was 'superior by eighteen fathoms [108 feet] to any pinnacle in the town, including that of the Church of Our Lady of Redcliffe'. During the reign of Henry VIII, who had

28 *The monumental Corinthian portico of the Victoria Rooms (1839–41) in Queen's Road. The Baroque fountain and the statue of Edward VII in full Garter robes were added* c. *1911.*

little time for pietistic practices, the chapel was demolished, and a Mr Read set up a windmill in its place in 1565. The Corporation acquired the hill in 1625 in order to 'keep it well prepared, maintaining the hedges and bushes and admitting the drying of clothes by townsmen and townswomen as had anciently been accustomed'. In the year of Victoria's Diamond Jubilee, it was decided to honour John Cabot, the voyager who sailed from Bristol and discovered Newfoundland. The result was the Tudor Gothic folly known as Cabot Tower (*front cover*), surmounted by the winged and gilded figure of Commerce holding a boat. The climb to the top of the 105-foot-high tower is a fair haul, but one is rewarded with splendid views, and a plan that identifies the main landmarks. The beautifully laid out rockeries, lily ponds, gardens and cascades make the hill a favourite retreat of summer strollers and students. The old notice, stipulating no carpet beating before 6 am or after 9 pm, is an interesting curiosity.

The walk from the top of Brandon Hill down into Brandon Hill Lane makes a pleasant approach to Berkeley Square, one of Bristol's modest Georgian showpieces. The houses were built in 1787 for those well-to-do citizens who wished to live between elegant Clifton and commercial Bristol. Although the enterprise faltered in the 1790s, owing to the Napoleonic Wars, it picked up

29 *The impressive Italianate range (c. 1855) by Foster and Wood in Queen's Road, the Bond Street of Bristol: an excellent early example of a purpose-built 'shopping parade'.*

afterwards and achieved tranquil respectability. At No. 7, John Addington Symonds (see p. 82) was born, and the great road-surfacer John Loudon McAdam, general surveyor of the Bristol Turnpike Trust, lived at No. 23. On a central patch of railinged grass, the copy of the old High Cross (see p. 69), very crocketed and intricate, stands like a regal reminder of more sternly devotional times.

From the south side of the square, near Brandon Hill Lane, there is a good view of the University Tower in Queen's Road (**26**). It was financed by the Wills family, designed by Sir George Oatley and finished in 1925. This most impressive structure, a looming shaft of assertive Gothicism, bears a considerable weight of classical erudition: the Muses Calliope (epic poetry), Thaleia (comedy and pastoral poetry), Urania (astronomy), Polyhymnia (sacred song), Clio (history), Erato (love songs), Euterpe (lyric poetry), Melpomene (tragedy) and Terpsichore (dance) are carved in full relief above the doorway. The bell in the tower, Great George, weighs 9½ tons and has an E-flat chime of pulverising loudness. After the tower's soaring bombast, the entrance hall does not disappoint: its 72-foot-high walls and majestic staircase create an effect 'as spectacular as its opposite number in Beckford's Fonthill', observed Pevsner, 'and three times as solid'.

The University (founded 1876) received its full charter in 1909. It has nearly 7,000 full-time students, 800 postgraduates and approximately 17,000 students on extra-mural courses. There are seven faculties: medicine, arts, science, law, engineering, social sciences and education.

The City of Bristol Museum and Art Gallery (**26, 30**) stands next door to the University. It has a spacious marbled interior, vaulted and broken by pillars and by galleries containing hosts of diverse artefacts: Egyptian painted coffins, Far Eastern lacquerware, Japanese ceramics, ivory ornaments, and paintings by Delacroix, Seurat and Renoir among others. The impressive local collection features such talents as Francis Danby, Samuel Jackson and J. B. Pyne, whose *Clifton from Ashton Meadows 1836* catches the misty indistinctness of morning light in a manner comparable to Corot's.

The Bristol district has a most varied geology, and the profusion of fossil casts, Mendip minerals and models of Ice Age mammals contribute to one particularly rewarding collection. The New Gallery of Natural History in West Britain shows birds in their normal habitats and plays recordings of their calls.

During the Second World War, the greater part of the Old Bristol Museum (next door to the present one) was destroyed, but the buff and red stone façade, modelled on the Doge's Palace at Venice, still survives and now fronts the University Refectory (**26**). The design of the local architects John Foster and Archibald Ponton (1872), it remains a rather slavish tribute to the genius of John Ruskin.

Queen's Road is Victorian and definitely unsedate, with fashion-conscious shops, banks and a post office. This main route through the city is dominated by the crushing Corinthian portico of the Victoria Rooms (now owned by the University). Completed in 1841 as a public hall and political meeting place, it has a striking pediment (by Jabez Tyley) showing Athena riding in a chariot driven by Apollo, attended by nymphs and graces (**28**). Charles Dickens gave readings here (1866–9) and the Irish apostle of decadence, Oscar Wilde, lectured on aesthetics. The forecourt creates a most active composition: a

30 *The light and spacious entrance hall of the City Museum and Art Gallery is just wide enough to accommodate this replica of a Bristol Biplane, one of three built for the film* Those Magnificent Men in their Flying Machines. *Also known as the Bristol Boxkite, this type of aircraft was the first to go into quantity production. About 75 were built from 1910 onwards, initially at the Brislington works of the Bristol Tramways and Carriage Company and later at the British and Colonial Aeroplane Company at Filton. The Bristol Boxkite was based on a design by the French aviator Henri Farman, and was used to train pilots in the early years of the First World War.*

Baroque fountain tricked out with shoals of aquatic deities and creatures – a Triton, a Nereid, flying-fishes, shells, seaweed and a sealion eating a fish. By contrast the statue of Edward VII in full Garter robes looks ultra-pompous.

Prominent from the Victoria Rooms is the Royal West of England Academy in Whiteladies Road, whose magnificent domed and Grecian interior provides a venue for art exhibitions, including a popular open one, held every autumn. The façade (1855–8), by J. H. Hirst, is very much an Italian Renaissance concept, exemplified by ground-floor rustication and columns flanking first-floor Venetian windows (**32**). It was erected as a permanent gallery in which Bristol artists could exhibit, and also to remove from the city the stigma of 'neglecting those arts which are the result of and evidence of a high state of civilisation'.

Bristol Grammar School (**31**), to the east, is bounded by University and Elton Roads and has the distinction of being one of the oldest established schools in the city, with an impressive academic record. The new premises of the institution were designed in 1877, and it is thought that the headmaster, J. W. Caldicott, was recalling his old school building (King Edward VI Grammar School at Birmingham by Sir Charles Barry) when he chose the

31 *The Gothic Great Hall of Bristol Grammar School (1879), designed by Foster and Wood.*

32 *The Royal West of England Academy (1855–8) provides a permanent venue for art exhibitions in Bristol. The rusticated ground-floor façade was added in 1912.*

Perpendicular Gothic mode. Even if the style is predictable, a certain liveliness is created by the mixture of pink rubble and Bath stone. The school itself was founded by Robert and Nicholas Thorne in 1532 (when wealthy merchants tended to fund charities and educational establishments rather than entrusting all their money to the church), 'for boys to be taught in good manners and literature'. Its companion grammar school, Queen Elizabeth's Hospital, now situated at the top of Jacob's Wells Road, was founded in 1586 by John Carr, a soap-boiler, and is renowned for the Elizabethan garb still worn by its boarding pupils.

5. The Harbour, Queen Square and St Mary Redcliffe

Dominating the waterfront of St Augustine's Reach is Broad Quay House, built for the Standard Life Assurance Company in 1981–2. This creative adaptation of the Victorian commercial style, varied by Velux windows and a hexagonal domed roof sitting on it tightly like a soldier's helmet, does much to vindicate modern architecture.

In its shadow stands the statue of Neptune (**34**) cast by the Bristol founder John Rendall in 1723. Originally conceived as an ornamental flourish to a new water supply in Temple Street, the figure, standing on the back of a dolphin, looks suitably hoary-bearded and patriarchal, although the plump sleekness of his pot belly suggests the laxity of a voluptuary rather than the moody energy of the sea king.

Bryan Little observed that one of the most pleasing policies of the Bristol

35 The Watershed Media Centre, created out of moribund dockside transit sheds in the early 1980s, and nowadays vibrant with new life even at night.

33 *Samuel Plimsoll (1824–98), beside the Avon Gorge in Hotwells. This social reformer was born in Bristol and became MP for Derby. He is best known today for inventing the Plimsoll Mark, which prevents ships from being dangerously overloaded.*

34 *This statue of Neptune, the god of the sea, appropriately guards the head of St Augustine's Reach.*

City Council has been the refurbishing of late-Georgian and early-Victorian warehouses. The Watershed Media Centre, on the west side of St Augustine's Reach, is an outstanding example of this enlightened transformation of 'moribund waterside buildings' into structures of utility and elegance (**35**). It offers two modern cinemas, galleries, darkrooms, workshops and a bar and restaurant area. The decorative endpiece, with its polygonal tower topped by a dome, was designed by Edward Gabriel. It dates from 1894 when the Port Authorities decided to give E shed a more attractive aspect, so that it would complement rather than distract from the elegance of College Green. The transit sheds south of the Watershed have been converted into the Bristol Exhibition Centre. This is the venue not only for the local motor show and the Women's World Exhibition but also for the World Wine Fair, an eight-day event which draws over eighty thousand people every July. The *Lochiel*, a twin-screwed motor vessel moored here, is now a floating bar and restaurant; in its previous existence it transported mail along the Glasgow–West Loch–Tarbert–Islay route.

Another excellent example of the redevelopment of the harbour area can be seen in the sensitive treatment accorded to the Arnolfini, a warehouse begun in 1832 for Acraman's, a firm of merchants and ships' chandlers. R. S. Pope was the architect. He provided the building with cast-iron Doric columns (later removed) and furnished it in high Victorian style. Later the warehouse was used for storing tea, but fell victim to London competition. In 1957 it was converted to its present use, housing a bookshop, cinema, art gallery (**38**) and theatre. This is Bristol's modern cultural nucleus and the envy of many other cities. The prize-winning sculpture above the entrance is a not very substantial framework of tubes, like the bones of a kite, but it does flash pink, mauve and green. A new statue of John Cabot was erected on the quayside outside the gallery in 1985 (**36**).

Close to the Arnolfini, the Prince Street swing bridge spans the Floating Harbour (see p. 62). The Grove, an old quay where formerly sand and timber were unloaded, turns off east from this point. At the bridge end stands the Clipper, a modern pub converted from an old seed warehouse, while at the other end, also on the corner, the Hole in the Wall draws numerous patrons. An 18th-century tavern, alleged to be the inspiration for the 'Spyglass' described by Robert Louis Stevenson in *Treasure Island*, it overlooks the waterside, and there are narrow slits in its walls set at eye-level, a definite asset when the press gang was prowling around looking for sailors. From here there is an excellent view of the colour-washed houses on Redcliffe Parade.

The expansive Queen Square, north of the Grove, takes its name from Queen Anne, who visited the city in 1702. Its construction (1699–1727) necessitated the draining of the old Marsh, formerly a place of bear-baiting,

36 *John Cabot of Venice settled in Bristol in c. 1495, and left from there to discover Newfoundland. This new statue, set into the cobbles on Narrow Quay in 1985, shows him gazing over the water of the Floating Harbour.*

37 *Rysbrack's monument to William III in the centre of Queen Square; erected in 1736 by the Bristol Whigs, it shows him in heroic style, riding stirrupless.*

archery and military exercises. The scale of the square, allegedly the largest in England after London's Lincoln's Inn Fields, makes the houses seem fairly modest, their outlook softened by lawns and spreading plane trees. Many are now offices for the better-paid professions, but in the past leading Bristol merchants occupied these properties. Hence the square became a target for the mob during the riots of 1831 (see pp. 15, 17). The centre, now unfortunately bisected by the ring road (1935), is dominated by Rysbrack's equestrian statue (1732–5; **37**) of William III. He looks imperious, fearless in Roman armour, and rides stirrupless in the classical manner. His horse, too, looks muscular and seems endowed with thoroughbred impulsion.

Associations throng around the square. The philosopher David Hume worked at No. 16 in 1734 and was sacked for correcting his employer's English. 'I have made £20,000 by my English', he was told, 'and I will not have it mended.' Edmund Burke lived at No. 19 during the 1774 election. At No. 37 the Polish patriot Kosciuszko stayed in June 1797 as a guest of the first American consul, Mr Vanderhorst. A great revolutionary hero in his time, he visited Bristol while on his way to America. He was locally called the 'Pocket Patriot', being below average size yet much venerated by Bristolians for his 'exalted genius . . . intrepid valour and warlike coolness against the bonds of haughty, presumptuous and sanguinary tyrants'. No. 29 (1709–11) is remarkable not only for its showiness, displaying Tuscan, Ionic and Corinthian columns, but also for being the birthplace of Richard Bright, 19th-century pioneer of kidney medicine. It is one of the few remaining unaltered early-18th-century houses in the square.

38 *An exhibition in the Arnolfini Gallery on Narrow Quay, a famous showcase for new developments in the arts.*

Queen Square lies south of King Street, which was laid out in 1663, just outside the 13th-century extension to the town wall. It has a very special old-world feel to it: a medley of red brick, stone, black and white timbering, cobbles and classical façades, with splashes of strong colour – ochre, red and blue. At the west end are the pink-painted Merchant Venturers' Almshouses (**6**). Intended as homes for retired seamen, they look very shipshape with their pedimented entrances and railinged courtyard. They originally made a quadrangle and were rebuilt as such in 1696–9, but one side was razed during the blitz. Next door is the Old Library (1739), now a restaurant, built on land described as 'one little messuage . . . adjacent to the Town Wall on the edge of the Marsh', donated by the citizen Robert Redwood in 1613. The first library having become dilapidated, the books were removed to the Council House, and a new building was begun to a design by James Paty. Palladian in character, it was decorated with baroque plaques showing naked boys frisking about among learned tomes and scientific and musical instruments – but these were removed in the 1950s, owing to their decayed state. The King Street Library continued to function until early this century, when the collection was transferred to College Green. Coleridge and Southey looked upon it as a kind of literary anchor and used it regularly. The Old Library's neighbour is the Bunch of Grapes, a favoured pub standing on the site of an

39 *The Llandoger Trow in King Street, converted from three 17th-century houses, is named after the flat-bottomed sailing barges that used to berth in Welsh Back. The granite setts and pennant pavements were relaid on one level in the early 1980s as part of a civic pedestrianisation scheme.*

40 *The ceiling of the Theatre Royal auditorium, designed by James Paty in imitation of Sir Christopher Wren's Drury Lane theatre, retains the original colour scheme of gold and green.*

OVERLEAF

41 *The Granary (1871), the last remaining warehouse building on Welsh Back, is a spectacular example of the colourful variegated brick and stone style known as Bristol Byzantine; it is now a rock-music centre.*

42 *The soaring 292–foot spire of St Mary Redcliffe (a 19th-century replacement of the medieval original), seen across the water from the Grove.*

earlier tavern dating from 1762. The frontage belongs to a former Victorian warehouse and the conversion has marked gaiety and elan.

The Theatre Royal (opened 1766) adds lustre to King Street. This was one of the earliest and best provincial theatres, and duly opposed by the Puritan element, who criticised staged entertainment as morally subversive and as 'promoting the arts of intrigue and seducing the innocent'. But the Theatre Royal has given pleasure to generations of audiences. Many famous actors and actresses have performed here, including Sarah Siddons, Grimaldi, Henry Irving, Ellen Terry, Edmund and Charles Kean and William Charles Macready, and here the talents of such playwrights as Harold Pinter, John Arden, Peter Nichols and Tom Stoppard have been fostered and launched. The Georgian auditorium provides a sumptuous show of gilded elegance. The early interior was all of wood, but fire destroyed it in 1800. Convex fluted Doric columns and plaster stars on the ceiling create a festive atmosphere (**40**). The foyer incorporates the Palladian hall of the Guild of Coopers (1743), an association of barrel-makers who chiefly produced casks for sugar, wine and rum. This alteration entailed a skilful extension, carried out in 1972, when the New Vic was added – a versatile studio theatre, which presents both new and established playwrights – and the basement was converted into the cloakroom and bar.

On the corner of King Street and Queen Charlotte Street are St Nicholas' Almshouses (1652), preserving part of the old town wall in the courtyard. This was the first building to be put up in the street; it was restored in 1961 and converted into flats.

51

The spirituous grandee hereabouts is the Llandoger Trow (**39**), a swaggering complex of bars converted from three timber-framed 17th-century houses and taking its name from the flat-bottomed sailing barges that berthed in Welsh Back (see below). The gables and projecting windows – all striped and crossed with black beams – create a picture of comfortable intimacy. One can understand why this famous pub, with its histrionic hints of cutlass-brandishing and baccy-chewing, is alleged to have served as a model for the 'Admiral Benbow' in R. L. Stevenson's *Treasure Island*. Opposite the Llandoger is the Old Duke, a jazz-lover's paradise and very popular – on certain evenings procuring a drink requires fortitude and physical audacity.

The bizarre Granary (1871; **41**), a landmark at the corner of Little King Street and Queen Charlotte Street, exemplifies the colourful variegated brick and stone style that has come to be called 'Bristol Byzantine'. Eight storeys high, with a fishtail ornament around the parapet, its neurotic ornateness is perhaps appropriate to its present function as a rock-music centre.

Little King Street emerges into Welsh Back, an old quay retaining memories of the many Welsh sailing barges, laden with coal and other goods, that docked here. This was part of the old port where the Avon flowed before the harbour complex was developed. Merchants' houses crowded up to the river, vantage points for close observation of the progress of their investments. A pair of 18th-century cannons are inset into the cobbles, and cannon barrels left over from the Civil War serve as capstans. The quay lost something of its 'decayed Hanseatic air' when the 19th-century warehouses were converted into studios and apartments, but it has gained a new functionalism.

A dominant feature of eastern dockland is the sky-defying outline of St Mary Redcliffe (**42**), praised by Queen Elizabeth I as the 'fairest, goodliest and mot famous parish church in England'. Four centuries later, despite being lassoed by a complex of busy roads, it still looks noble and imposing, its flying buttresses and openwork parapet of triangles crowned by the 293-foot spire, which was lopped off by lightning in 1445 and replaced in 1872. This triumph of high Gothicism began as the Norman shrine of Our Lady of Redcliffe and developed through succeeding periods until the end of the 14th century, when the main body of the building was completed.

The inner north porch (c. 1200) is a fine piece of Early English craftsmanship, showing pillars of black Purbeck marble, their capitals carved with characteristic crispness and verve (**43**). The hexagonal outer north porch is an outstanding achievement of Decorated work, surpassing all other examples of this rare form of approach to a church. The eye is dazzled by the variety, density and delicacy of carved decoration. The muniment room, housed above (not open to the public), is associated with the boy poet Thomas Chatterton (1752–70), whose birthplace (a curiously displaced slice of Georgiana with a triangular pediment), now a branch of the City Museum, lies across Redcliffe Way. Chatterton's father was a master at Redcliffe Charity School and died before his birth. The lonely, introspective child grew up in the shadow of St Mary and ingested the dust of its mouldering tombs, drawing the rarified atmosphere of past ages into his soul. He fell in love with archaic script, copied it, and produced forgeries and half-jocular legends. His ingenious Rowley poems almost baited the perspicacious Horace Walpole into accepting them as genuine, but the poet Thomas Gray detected the flaws. Dropped by Walpole, Chatterton rushed to London, desperate with ambition,

43 *The inner north porch (c. 1200) of St Mary Redcliffe.*

54

brimming with talent and enthusiasm and subsisting on little more than stale bread and water. Although he sent home pretty gifts to his mother and sister, his body was wasting and pride corroding under the smart of rejection and non-payment. Finally he was driven to buy arsenic and eat it. He expired painfully and his death brought him the renown and fame that had eluded him in life.

St Mary's nave is famous for its all-stone roof, which had to be rebuilt after the tower fell onto it during the storm of 1446. The ribbed vaulting branches out from over 1,200 stone bosses, all overlaid with gold that was donated in the 18th century, so the story goes, by the ladies of Bristol, who had their jewellery melted down for the purpose. Yet the effect is far from festive or gaudy, decorativeness being held at bay by the forest of slim piers that endow the church with a hushed twilit quality (**45**).

The renowned benefactor of St Mary, William Canynges the Younger, funded this rebuilding as well as the clerestory. Five times Mayor, twice Member of Parliament for the city, he is honoured by two monuments in the south transept. In one he lies in red and black merchant's robes in a four-poster tomb beside his wife (**44**); in the other he is clad as a priest – he took holy orders after his wife's death and became Dean of Westbury. Canynges' renown prompted the tradition of 'Rush Sunday', inaugurated in 1493 to commemorate his first celebration of the Holy Eucharist, on Whitsunday 1468. Each year, on Whitsunday, the church is strewn with rushes, nosegays of flowers decorate the pews, and the Lord Mayor and Corporation of Bristol attend the service in civic attire.

The baptistery, near the south porch, houses an octagonal medieval font

44 *The tomb erected in St Mary Redcliffe by its chief benefactor, William Canynges, for his wife Joanna, who died in 1467.*

45 *The lofty nave of St Mary Redcliffe, looking east.*

46 *Merchants Landing, part of the harmonious new housing development created along the waterfront of Bathurst Basin.*

built into the pillar, and the wall of the tower opposite bears the memorial tablet to Admiral Sir William Penn (d. 1670), father of the founder of Pennsylvania, together with his flags and armour. Beneath the tower, the Chapel of St John the Baptist (also known as the American Chapel because the Friends of St Mary Redcliffe in the United States restored and furnished it) contains a painted wooden statue of Queen Elizabeth I (probably a ship's figurehead), a superb wrought-iron screen (1710), which originally stretched across the nave, by William Edney, and a whalebone that John Cabot might have brought back from his voyage in 1497.

A less tragic memory than that of Thomas Chatterton is provided by the simple tombstone in the graveyard, outside the south transept, marked 'The Church Cat – 1912–1927'. This commemorates a frequenter of the church who befriended Ralph Morgan, organist during the 1920s and 1930s. She was reportedly a very musical cat, and would sit quietly on his lap while he practised in the choir.

In the church wall of St Mary, on Redcliffe Hill just north of Colston Parade, is a conduit given to the church in 1190 by Lord Robert de Berkeley. Each year, usually on the first Sunday in October, the clergy process along the whole length of the pipe to its source in Knowle in a kind of 'beating the bounds' ceremony. The walk entails forays into private gardens and usually provides many moments of light relief. Such rites, once common all over England, sought to instil consciousness of property and boundaries. This version is also a perpetual thank-offering to Berkeley himself, whose chain-mailed effigy lies in the north transept of the church.

Parallel with the south side of the church is Colston Parade. Here is Fry's House of Mercy (1784), almshouses for eight poor women. The plaque on No. 9 commemorates Samuel Plimsoll (b. 1824; **33**), who devised the famous line along ships' bows which regulates the quantity of cargo, and transformed 'floating coffins' into relatively reliable vessels.

Crossing Redcliffe Hill from the church and passing into Redcliffe Parade, one is almost straightaway plunged into silence, the awareness of traffic fading as the atmosphere of this silent cobbled street closes round. The delicate-toned 18th-century houses, which look over the water to the Grove, are perhaps best seen from there, jutting dramatically from the ruddy clifftop. Beneath them, honeycombing the sandstone, is a network of caverns which has aroused much conjecture. Were they for quarrying sand to make glass? Were they for contraband storage? Were they secret hiding places of felons? Organised parties are conducted round them by appointment with the City Engineer.

Redcliffe Parade is endowed with its own little garden, dating back to 1665, when Charles II granted the plot to the Society of Friends to be used as a burial ground. It has a cave called St John's Hermitage, lived in by a succession of anchorites from 1346 to 1669, when this area was meadowy and cattle-grazed. The garden is now set aside for the blind, and is redolent with herbs and attractive flowers. Steps lead down from the western end of Redcliffe Parade to Phoenix Wharf, where there is a late-19th-century hand crane. The adjoining Redcliffe Wharf is at present used as a local authority

47 Prince's Wharf: the Bristol Industrial Museum (opened in 1978), and beyond it the National Lifeboat Museum.

depot and is closed to the public, but there are plans to develop this area as a tourism and leisure centre.

South-west of Redcliffe Parade, Bathurst Basin, one of the three entrances to the Floating Harbour from the Avon, forms part of fashionable dockland, with neat neo-Georgian apartments in dark red brick as well as older colour-washed houses commanding a waterside view over sleek cruisers and motorboats. A favourite drinkers' rendezvous is the nearby Ostrich, an 18th-century inn with a patio on the waterfront and sandstone caves at the back which reputedly link up with St Mary Redcliffe. Smugglers, again, are said to have used the passages to hoard their contraband. The Smugglers Tavern, at the junction of Wapping and Cumberland Roads, is a Regency inn with a painting on its façade depicting a barrel-carrying felon – all in the best yo-ho-ho tradition.

Prince's Wharf is the site of the Bristol Industrial Museum (**47**), opened in 1978, and the National Lifeboat Museum. A transit shed houses various objects from the city's history including the world's oldest steam-driven car (1875), the Wanderer caravan (1885), Bristol cars of the 1940s, Douglas motorcycles and Rolls Royce aero-engines. The mock-up of the nose section of Concorde makes a fascinating fragment of aeronautic history, while the new gallery, which traces the history of the city docks and re-creates a 19th-century marine workshop, should be viewed in conjunction with the Maritime Heritage Centre, further west at Wapping Wharf.

Between the two is the Fairbairn Steam Crane, designed by Sir William Fairbairn (1789–1874) for raising heavy cargo from the deep holds of sailing ships. This particular model can lift 35 tons; it was built in 1876 by the Bath firm Stothert and Pitt, and has a central swivel post sunk deep into the dock.

Further west along the wharf (vehicular access from Gasferry Road) is the Maritime Heritage Centre. It came into being when the shipbuilding company of Charles Hill and Sons closed down, leaving a spectacular legacy of ship models, marine architects' drawings, paintings, prints and nautical instruments. A move was made to secure this unique collection for Bristol, aided by generous grants from various bodies, including Harveys. The result was the Maritime Heritage Centre, opened by the Queen in July 1985. Central to the display is the full-size copy of the BD6, a famous dredger designed by Brunel for the dispersal of mud from the city harbour. The ship was scrapped in 1962 but the engine has been cleaned and restored. Visitors can actually enter the hull and watch a video programme explaining the city's pioneering role in nautical history.

The Maritime Heritage Centre is also the entry point for the star attraction of Wapping Wharf, the SS *Great Britain* (**48** and *back cover*), Brunel's successor to the wooden paddle steamer the *Great Western*. This wrought-iron ship, the first to be fitted with a screw propeller, was launched in the presence of Prince Albert in 1843. After completing four return crossings of the Atlantic, she ran aground on the coast of Ireland and was salvaged a year later. She then took on a new career, shipping passengers to Australia, which she sustained for 23 years. In 1882 she was converted to a sailing ship but four years later the turbulent seas off Cape Horn drove her to the Falkland Islands where, damaged beyond feasible repair, she ended up as a storage hulk for coal and wool. In 1970, amid great publicity, she was towed back to Bristol and a rolling programme of restoration was begun which is still a topic of great

48 *Brunel's SS* Great Britain, *the first large ship to be constructed of iron and fitted with a screw propellor, now being restored in the dry dock from which she was launched in 1843.*

interest. Just one example of what has already been painstakingly achieved is the restored bow with a reproduction of the ship's figurehead, which includes the thunderbolt of Jove, indicating power, and the winged staff of Mercury, symbolising speed. To recapture something of the style of the *Great Britain*, there is the advertising handbill of 1861:

49 *A row of pretty cottages (1831) gives a village atmosphere to the middle of the Cumberland Basin.*

> This magnificent and far-famed Ship, fitted with oscillating engines, is the most celebrated Steamer afloat. Her last passage to Melbourne was made in 62 days, and the previous one in 55 days 16 hours, and back to Queenstown in 59 days . . . Her Saloon arrangements are perfect, and combine every possible convenience, – Ladies' Boudoir, Baths, &c., and her noble passenger decks, lighted at intervals by sideports, afford unrivalled accommodation for all classes.

At the western end of the dock complex is the Cumberland Basin, traditionally the main entrance to the Floating Harbour. This was the brainchild of William Jessop (1745–1814), who had a fresh channel dug for the Avon known as the 'New Cut' and dammed it on the site of the present Underfall Yard, leaving the ships 'floating' between the tides. Here is the girder-type swing bridge (1925) and the Italianate hydraulic engine house. This whole area is a treasury of maritime engineering and deserves close study. Two charming rows of cottages (**49**), one dated 1831, enhance the aspect of the Underfall Yard – which was originally called the Overfall Yard (because water flowed over the dam from the floating harbour), before Brunel himself had culverts fixed lower down to draw off the surplus.

6. The Saxon Core

This part of the city is historically most important, for it represents the first extension of Bristol into a significant town as opposed to merely the site of a powerful moated fortress. Four streets – High Street, Corn Street, Wine Street, Broad Street – were the nucleus of the Saxon walled town.

St Nicholas Street, on the southern edge of this area, north-west of Bristol Bridge, traces the line of a medieval thoroughfare and has a fountain to Queen Victoria (1859), almost rococo in style, with dimpled cherubs enclosing a scalloped niche. Further along is an exceptionally attractive inn called The Elephant (**51**), resplendently painted in scarlet and cream with the sculpture of a Jumbo clutching leaves in his trunk. St Nicholas' Church was rebuilt 1763–9 over the rib-vaulted crypt of a medieval church, whose chancel lay above a city gateway linking up with Bristol Bridge. Sections of the old 15-foot-thick city wall are incorporated in the south wall of the crypt, which is now a Brass Rubbing Centre; here visitors can produce a splendid copy of an armoured knight for a modest fee. The Georgian church was begun by the architect James Bridges, an American colonial by birth, who created an appropriate 15th-century Gothic design. The tall spire and western tower were the slightly later work of Thomas Paty. A bombing raid in 1940 gutted the building but services continued to be held in the crypt until 1959. Subsequently the church was restored, with the addition of a western gallery, to make a splendid museum of local history and ecclesiastical art. It houses Hogarth's famous altarpiece triptych (c. 1755), showing the Sealing of the Tomb, the Three Marys waiting, and the Ascension. Originally designed for St Mary Redcliffe, the painting was removed from there in the mid-19th century, when there was a general reaction against 'Georgian improvements'. The crypt contains the tomb of Alderman John Whitson, who promoted Pring's 1603 voyage to New England (see pp. 66, 69) and in 1634 founded Red Maids' School for 'forty poor women's children to be under the care of some woman and taught to read English, to sew and do other laudable work'.

Across St Nicholas Street are the covered markets, completed in 1745 as a fruit and vegetable trading area. These have been extended to include meat, poultry, fish, ironmongery, jewellery, books and paintings. The enclosure has the slightly grubby fascination characteristic of such places – always the hint of that elusive bargain hanging in the air – and the numerous interconnecting alleyways, such as Exchange Avenue and All Saints' Lane, give a sense of anticipation to all the wheeling and dealing.

All Saints' Court, which joins up with High Street, is on the northern side of St Nicholas' Markets. At the corner is the 17th-century glebe house of All

50 *Lloyds Bank (1854), Corn Street, inspired by Sansovino's Library in Venice and exuberantly decorated with sculpture by John Thomas (who worked also on the Houses of Parliament).*

51 *The Elephant (c. 1866), St Nicholas Street.*

Saints' Church. The church itself dates from the early 12th century but was gutted by fire in 1446. Formerly the meeting-place of the medieval Guild of Kalendars and the base for the city's earliest public library, which belonged to them, it is now an Institute of Christian and Urban Studies. The western half preserves fine Norman work whereas the chancel is mainly modern. The tower, crowned by an elaborate cupola (added 1807), evokes shades of oriental opulence, but the interior is dark and subtly oppressive. Rysbrack's statue of Edward Colston is the chief ornament: he reclines on an Ionic monument by James Gibbs in a full-bottomed wig, his right hand clasping his breast – a gesture implying heartfelt compassion – and his face lined and world-weary, as if depleted by practising so much philanthropy.

One side of the church stands in Corn Street, a name evoking richness and fertility – aptly so, for this was Bristol's major banking street during the 18th and 19th centuries, and certain buildings have an almost overdressed classical panache. Lloyds Bank (1854; **50**) was inspired by Sansovino's Library in Venice and was the work of W. B. Gingell and T. R. Lysaght. The commercial spirit of Venice is translated in the frieze, which dynamically extols the poetry of profit. The figures symbolise the various sources of wealth: merchants are shown trading with exotic natives and putti mint coins and print bank notes. The Corn Exchange (1743) dominates the pedestrianised area of Corn Street, flanked by the four equidistant Nails (**52**). These dish-shaped brass tables were used by merchants to complete their transactions – hence the saying 'to pay on the nail'. In the 17th century they were incorporated in a colonnade known as the Exchange, or Tolzey, which formed the main open-air bartering place in England's second city. Exposed to the blown dust and constant clamour of the street, it was not the most sedate place. The number of merchants and traders grew steadily and by the 18th century the City Council was debating the construction of 'a place in the nature of an Exchange'. John Wood, the Palladian genius of Bath, was eventually commissioned to do the work. He produced a suitably majestic design with a rusticated arched base and a pediment supported by lofty Corinthian columns. This imposing façade concealed a gracious colonnaded piazza, which made up the central section. At first Bristolians were 'startled with the novelty' of trading under cover, and the piazza, then open to the sky, was perhaps a nostalgic nod to the past. Nevertheless, after the 1740s it was fitted with an iron-framed glass roof. The Corn Street paving and furnishing scheme was completed as the city's contribution to European Architectural Heritage Year (1975).

The Commercial Rooms (1810–11, by A. Busby), further down on the opposite side of the street, were inspired by Lloyd's Coffee House in London. John Wood's Exchange, despite its grandeur, did not prove popular as a merchants' meeting-place. A more relaxed atmosphere, akin to that of a coffee house or club, was favoured during the Regency period, and the building of the Rooms reflected the mood of commercial well-being which followed the completion of the Floating Harbour. The graceful Ionic façade, crowned by figures symbolising the City, Commerce and Navigation, is an extraordinarily effective adaptation of the Greek mode, and avoids the bombast of the Victoria Rooms (see pp. 42, 44). The interior has a beautiful skylight supported by a circle of caryatids, providing a fitting climax to the ornamental Georgian plasterwork, framed panelling and coved ceiling.

Corn Street merges into Clare Street, another treasury of ambitious Victorian architecture. The terracotta former Prudential building (1899, by Alfred Waterhouse), is a bizarre marriage of the Flemish and Scottish Baronial styles, with a mountain of a chimney stack. No. 15 (1889) complements this exterior with a design by Henry Edwards in buff and reddish stone, with fancy-dress flourishes in late Queen Anne style.

St Stephen's Street, separating Clare Street from Corn Street, traces the curve of the old medieval wall. The former *Bristol Times and Mirror* building (1904) is a half-timbered effusion in Arts and Crafts style; more spectacular is the building by the turning into Colston Avenue known as Quay Head House (1884, by John Foster and Joseph Wood), tricked out with such fine details as urn-crowned balustrading and a pilastered and pedimented gable of the Flemish variety.

The intricate traceried tower of St Stephen's captivated John Ruskin, who called it 'one of the most stately gems of ecclesiastical art'. The church dates from 1440 and most of the fabric is Perpendicular Gothic. At the end of the north aisle is the monument to Martin Pring (d. 1626). The central tablet is

52 *The Exchange (1741), the only work in Bristol by John Wood of Bath. Two of the four Nails on which merchants formerly transacted their business can be seen here in front of the beautiful Palladian façade. The pedestrianisation of this part of Corn Street has completed its transformation from the hub of commerce to a leisurely piazza-like area.*

53 *This fine Baroque sword-rest in St Stephen's Church is the early-18th-century craftsmanship of William Edney, the famous Bristol smith whose work can also be seen in St Mary Redcliffe.*

inscribed with a verse panegyric; Grecian-robed attendants sit at the four corners and below are a merman, a mermaid, and an anchor, scythe and hourglass (symbols of mortality), with the signature of the carver, W. R. Pugh. In 1603 Pring sailed to New England under licence from Sir Walter Ralegh, anchoring in Whitson Harbour, later called Plymouth (USA) by the Pilgrim Fathers. He was made General of the West Indies and was brought back to Bristol when he died. His wife, Hannah Oliver, put up this memorial to him. There is an equally fine monument to the appropriately recumbent Edmond Blanket (c. 1370), a wool merchant jestingly credited with the invention of bed covering. He wears a tight-fitting hose, cape, tunic with a 'cote hardie', and a jewel-encrusted belt. The belt denotes his wealth and status: Edward III forbade the use of such belts to anyone below the rank of knight who did not possess £200.

The eastern end of Corn Street marks the meeting-point of the four major streets of the old town: High Street, Corn Street, Wine Street and Broad Street. Here stood the old High Cross (1373), 40 feet high and elaborately traceried with the statues of kings in the niches. It was said to sway during high winds, and a frightened goldsmith who lived nearby complained that it might truncheon him and his wife to death. In the 18th century it was moved to College Green and in 1768 the Dean of Bristol gave it to Henry Hoare, lord of Stourhead, Wiltshire; there is a copy of the top part in Berkeley Square (see p. 42).

A plaque commemorating the High Cross is inset into the wall of the Old Council House, designed by Sir Robert Smirke (1822–7). Occupying the site of the medieval church of St Ewan, this is the descendant of a series of earlier civic buildings, notably the modest two-gabled original Council House which adjoined the colonnaded Tolzey. In 1699 the civic headquarters became the subject of criticism; something more palatial and commanding was required for a thriving city. The Council ordered the 'amendment and repair' of the building, but instead the Tolzey colonnade was demolished and a completely new Council House was erected in Queen Anne vernacular Baroque. When these premises were found inadequate for the expanding city, Smirke created a new building in the neoclassical mode, with fluted Ionic columns dominating the doorway and a central figure of Justice gazing down from the high balustrade – a structure of reassuring sobriety and balance rather than gaiety or lightness.

At the corner of High Street and Corn Street, the publisher and bookseller Joseph Cottle set up his business in 1794. An indifferent versifier himself, he was quick to recognise the precocious talents of Coleridge and Southey. He brought out their early work, visiting Coleridge and his wife Sara at their Clevedon home, and published early poems by Wordsworth, who wrote 'Lines Composed Above Tintern Abbey' in his parlour.

Wine-Street, the eastern continuation of Corn Street, sustained heavy losses during the blitz, including several early timbered merchants' houses and the splendid Dutch House, described as having a 'bank of windows like the stern galleries of a man o' war', which was reputedly brought piece by piece from Holland. Many of the old sites have been filled in with office blocks, one of them named Southey House after the poet, who was born at No. 9 in 1774 and christened at Christ Church. The son of a respected local linen-draper, he started out as something of a rebel, expelled from public school for writing an outspoken essay on corporal punishment. He co-operated with Coleridge on his pantisocratic venture (which never materialised), but in later years he settled for orthodoxy, ending up as Poet Laureate; he died in 1843. The road was originally called Wynch Street after a pillory which stood here; 'Wine' was a logical progression in view of Bristol's trade in that commodity.

Broad Street is paradoxically rather narrow; the buildings of many periods create a richly varied effect. The finest church here – one of the most distinctive in the city – is Christ Church, probably the work of William Paty (1786–90). The massive tower and spire are indebted to Wren; the Florentine west door strikes the right note of refined embellishment. The Georgian interior, saucer-domed, white and gold, with slender Corinthian columns, has a feel of cool opulence (**54**). Still the best-loved feature of the church are the quarterjacks on the outside. Red-kilted and blue-jacketed, they swing round every quarter of an hour, smiting the bells with their axes. James Paty carved them in 1728. Christ Church was still a medieval structure then but in 1786 it was pulled down in order that Wine Street could be widened. When the new church was built by James Paty's kinsman William, the quarterjacks were not replaced. Eventually they were traced to a Bath scrapyard and reinstated to their rightful perches in 1913.

Opposite the Grand Hotel (1869) is the old Bank of England (1844) by C. R. Cockerell. The frontage is Doric, with two entrance porches and gaunt round-headed windows. It emits a faintly funereal flavour, like an undertaker – financially secure, yet oppressed by his melancholy vocation.

The Guildhall (1846), now part of the Law Courts, replaced an earlier building where Bristol's civic dignitaries and the members of the most important guilds met and discussed their policies – a sketch of it can be seen in Millerd's map of the city (1673), showing it as an intricate essay in Tudor Gothic. This was where Judge Jeffries dealt out raw justice to the survivors of Monmouth's Rebellion in 1685. In 1839, a committee was set up to consider additions and improvements to the building, but the plan was abandoned in favour of demolition and a new Guildhall. R. S. Pope was the architect, choosing a more florid Elizabethan Gothic style with a central two-storeyed rectangular oriel over the entrance arch.

A turning north-east off Broad Street leads into Taylors' Court. Here is one of Bristol's lurking surprises: a very regal shell-hooded doorway, for what was formerly the Guild Hall of the Merchant Taylors (**55**). The hood contains a lively coat of arms, featuring two prancing camels (artistically horsified), John the Baptist (the guild's patron saint), a cherub's head with a winged collar and the motto 'Concordia Parvae Res Crescunt' ('Concord makes small things flourish'). The guild was formed in 1399 by a charter of Richard II and was one of 24 such guilds in the city, of which only the Merchant Venturers survives.

The jauntiest and most unusual building in Broad Street is Edward Everard's Printing House (**56**), near St John's Gateway. The ceramic decoration of Doulton Carrara (so called because it resembles marble) by W. J. Neatby produces a dance and dazzle of colour that seems almost an affront to the grey-skied old West Country port. Everard wrote in 1900, 'I am a printer heart and head and hand. Having in mind the century linking 1400 and 1500, when the daybreak of a new era was dawning out of the creation of Gutenberg, I elected to raise in Bristol a trophy contemporary with that

54 The splendid elegance of Christ Church (1786–90) has been maintained despite many alterations to the interior. The white and gold Georgian chancel screen was originally the altarpiece.

CONCORDIA PARVÆ RES CRESCUNT

period and with that genius. Coupled with this was the desire to repeat the salient features of St John's Gateway . . .' The tiled façade depicts the Spirit of Literature presiding over ancient and modern printing. Gutenberg and William Morris are shown slaving at the press and Everard's name appears on a bold blue ground. This is Art Nouveau's challenge to the spirit of cautious timidity, and when the building was opened, in 1901, police were needed to keep back the crowds who came to hoot or applaud or just goggle.

Closing the view down the street is the archway attached to St John's Church. Queen Elizabeth I rode on a white horse through this gateway when she visited the city in 1574. The portcullis groove of the old gate is still visible and the figures of Brennus and Belinus, legendary founders of Bristol, sit magisterially in their niches (1). The church was one of the four built on a section of the medieval town wall and its elegantly spired tower was originally shared with the small church of St Lawrence, pulled down in the 16th century. St John's has an ancient rib-vaulted crypt (entered from Nelson Street), but the church is essentially Perpendicular (c. 1380), without aisles owing to lack of space. The interior (open on Thursday afternoons) has a Jacobean font, some good Georgian paintings, a unique pulpit hourglass and the recumbent effigy of Walter Frampton (d. 1388), a rich merchant who financed the church.

Duck under the arch and turn right into Nelson Street to find St John's Conduit (at one time inside the gate and restored 1866), an intriguing old lion-spouted fountain. This harks back to the Middle Ages, when the overflow from the spring used by the Carmelite friary (where the Colston Hall stands now) was piped through Host Street and Christmas Street to the gateway, where by permission of the friars the parishioners of St John's were allowed to use the water. When the blitz cut off the water supply in this quarter in 1940, the citizens were once again able to rely on this traditional, unfailing source.

55 A magnificent shell-hood in Taylors' Court, off Broad Street, showing the coat of arms of the Mechant Taylors' Guild, which used to meet here; the motto means 'Concord Makes Small Things Flourish' (it appears again on p. 76).

56 The bright Art Nouveau ceramic façade of Edward Everard's Printing House depicts Johann Gutenberg (c. 1400–68), the first European to print with movable metal types; the Spirit of Literature; and William Morris, the English poet and craftsman who led the late-19th-century renaissance of fine printing.

7. Broadmead, Castle Park and Temple Meads

57 Unaccustomed calm in The Arcade, allowing a better view of the Ionic columns and shallow bow windows. It was originally one of a pair (1842–5) but its partner was destroyed during the blitz.

58 The shopping area of Castle Street and Wine Street, another victim of wartime air raids, has been replaced by this modern precinct in Broadmead.

Broadmead is now the city's major shopping centre, replacing the older one in Castle Street and Wine Street largely destroyed during the blitz. It caters for most conceivable requirements, and the shopping precinct (**58**), while not aesthetically entrancing, is spacious and bright, with plane trees, benches and the occasional guitarist or hurdy-gurdy grinder. The Arcade (**57**), leading through into the Horsefair, was built in 1824. Ionic columns loom at the entrance and the shallowly bow-fronted shops catch the willing eye. In the core of all this activity, like a stern rebuke, the mounted figure of John Wesley sits on his horse at the Broadmead entrance to the New Room, the first Methodist chapel in the world, opened in 1739 and extended towards Broadmead in 1748. Inside, Roman Doric pillars support the ceiling and the mahogany-finished box pews contrast with the white panelling. A particular treasure is the double-decker pulpit from which Wesley preached his soul-stirring sermons; the galleries are the original ones (**60**). At the Horsefair

entrance is a statue of Charles Wesley; wigged and clad in cassock and gown, he looks stern and unyielding as he wields a Bible in one hand and performs an exhortatory flourish with the other.

Behind the shops, in one of the service courts (between Merchant Street and Penn Street), is Quakers' Friars (**7**), an odd-sounding religious marriage. The friary was an old Dominican building, established before 1230 and dissolved in 1542. Over a hundred years later we find a prosperous grocer, Dennis Hollister (a lapsed Baptist who had 'sucked in some upstart doctrines'), giving the visiting Quaker preachers John Camm and John Audland a field 'in the Friars' for a meeting house. Here in 1670 the Quakers put up their early headquarters, utilising the old friary ruins; and here in 1696 William Penn, the founder of Pennsylvania, married Hollister's granddaughter. Today the Registry Office does its business in the early Quakers' meeting hall (a later building by George Tully, 1747), while the friary itself incorporates the Permanent Planning Exhibition – a prime reference source for the history of local changes. The Bristol Tapestry, also exhibited here, consists of four sections, each 18 feet by 4 feet, depicting in a bright naïve style the city's history over the last 1,000 years. This part of the friary (to add yet another historical stratum) is called the Bakers' and Cutlers' Hall, after the guild which met here in the period after the Dissolution.

From Quakers' Friars it is only a short distance into Merchant Street,

59 *Tucked away on the southern side of Merchant Street are the Merchant Taylors' Almshouses, restored by Lloyds Bank (see also p. 72).*

60 *The muted interior of the New Room offers a welcome respite from the bustle of the city centre. John Wesley, founder of the Methodist movement, preached from this beautiful double-decker pulpit to his congregation in the mahogany-topped box pews.*

formerly called Marshal Street, after the soldiers who took this route from the castle to their drill or assembly grounds on Kingsdown. Intensive bombing erased the old buildings here, with the exception of the Merchant Taylors' Almshouses (**59**), built in 1701 for nine poor tailors or their widows and daughters. Lloyds Bank have now taken these quarters in hand, doing a very thorough restoration which gained them a Civic Trust Award.

St James' Church tends to be overlooked because it is situated in that busy commercial area bounded by the Haymarket (until 1900 the actual hay markets were held in the churchyard) and Marlborough Street. The neighbouring bus station, from which the green-painted vehicles regularly emerge with much groaning and drawling, does little to heighten its appeal. The church is said to be the oldest in the city, occupying the site of the priory erected in 1130 by Robert, Earl of Gloucester, bastard son of Henry I. The priory belonged to Tewkesbury Abbey (which also owned the hermitage on Brandon Hill, see p. 40) and it comprised a cloister, dormitory, refectory and gatehouse. Certain parts of the Norman church remain, including a row of intersecting arches, surmounted by a charming interlaced early wheel window. The tomb effigy under an arch in the south wall, perhaps carved by a stonemason who had worked on Wells Cathedral, is of the founder, Robert (d. 1148).

South of the shopping precincts the salubrious retreat of Castle Park spreads itself out generously: an invigorating greensward planted with young trees and opened in 1976. It is dominated by the gutted shell of St Peter's Church (**62**), whose 13th-century tower has Norman work around the base. Across the water, smoke from the Courage brewery plumes out lazily, and the whole scene seems fitting and right. Devastation should not always be hastily concealed, and this site is the historic tap-root of the city. Here Bricgstow

began, and here archaeologists have uncovered Saxon houses that must predate the Norman castle, of which only the worn-down ramparts remain. The castle was an immense building, exerting dictatorial authority until the city centre moved away from it, to Corn Street and Wine Street, when the power of the merchant classes finally shook off the feudal stranglehold. Although this area was severely bombed in the blitz, St Mary-le-Port, at the south-western end of Castle Park, retains its fine 15th-century western tower. Excavation has shown that there was a church here in Norman time, perhaps even earlier.

An exhilarating sight from Castle Park is the Shot Tower (**61**) in Cheese Lane. This modernistic shaft of reinforced concrete was erected for the process of making lead shot; the molten metal is sieved through a perforated plate and dropped a great distance. The technique was perfected by William Watts, a Redcliffe plumber, who conducted his early experiments at home – which involved cutting holes in the floors and ceiling. In 1782 he tacked a tower on the roof of his house, which worked effectively; demand for shot grew, earning Watts a fortune which he quickly dispersed in property speculation. His tower was in use until 1969, when it was demolished and replaced by the present lofty edifice, designed by E. A. Underwood and Partners.

The River Avon flows alongside Castle Park and under Bristol Bridge, which now connects Victoria Street and High Street. This is not the famous old structure, which was crammed with houses and a chapel, but a Georgian replacement put up in 1769 by James Bridges, who shortly after left for the

61 *The Shot Tower, a striking modern landmark in Cheese Lane, beside the eastern end of the Floating Harbour.*

78

West Indies because he had got weary of the numerous disputes the bridge provoked. When all the ships came up and moored here, there must have been a veritable jungle of masts and rigging, but now the river is relatively shipless and free for the gulls to ride upon. Many new developments have arisen south of the river, and yet in a sense this bridge still marks a division, between prosperous Bristol and the more run-down area of Victoria Street and Temple Church, in Church Lane. The Knights Templar, an exclusive and aristocratic order of chivalry, founded a church on this site in about 1147, when Robert of Gloucester gave them the district known as Temple Fee. The Templars usually had round churches, modelled on the Church of the Holy Sepulchre in Jerusalem, but this one was oval. The remains of the present church, with tall arcades and a Baroque west doorway, date from the 1390s, but the outline of the Templars' church has been traced by excavation. The 114-foot tower leans at a drunken angle, not as a result of the bombing which destroyed the body of the church, but merely through age and subsidence. The church eventually became the parish church of this district, patronised by the weavers who lived in the area. The graveyard, which used to exude a forlorn lyricism, has been tidied up and given a substantial wall.

62 The 14th-century shell of St Peter's Church is a constant reminder of the bombs that fell on Bristol. The surrounding area of Castle Park, landscaped in 1976, forms an ideal setting for open-air concerts.

Temple Meads Station

In 1833 Isambard Kingdom Brunel was appointed engineer to a railway company planning to construct a line between Bristol and London. It took eight years to lay the 118 miles of track. A terminus had to be built for the

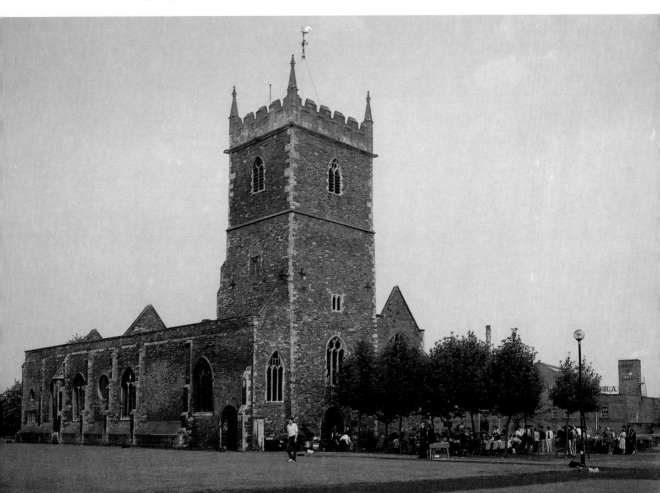

Great Western, as the railway was now called, and Brunel rose to the challenge. In 1839 he put up a massive enclosure of stone, brick, timber and cast iron, over 80 feet longer than Bristol Cathedral. This is the world's earliest surviving railway terminus. The façade (1839–40), a hectic Tudor-style concoction with angle turrets and a central oriel, facing Temple Gate on the north-west side of the station approach, is protected as a Grade 1 listed building.

In 1865 Temple Meads was reorganised as the main terminus for the three Bristol railways – the Great Western, the Midland and the Bristol and Exeter. At that early period, the station was a steam-lover's idyll, as an extract from *Morgan's Guide* (1849) suggests:

> A porter is ready to conduct you to the booking office, where you pay your fare and receive your ticket; you then ascend a flight of stairs to the platform. Having taken your place, and made all ready, you are now at ease to observe what is going on . . . several engines with red hot fires in their bodies, and volumes of condensed steam issuing from them: one of them moves slowly towards you. The huge piece bellows at first like an elephant: deep, slow and terrific are the hoarse heavings it makes. It is then linked to the carriages . . . a whistle is sounded for starting – and then you are off.

Brunel's great train shed also survives (**63**). It was last used by trains in 1965, and then British Rail donated it to the Brunel Engineering Centre Trust; adorned with its maker's statue at one end, it remains a masterly example of aesthetic functionalism.

63 *The remarkable mock hammerbeam roof of Brunel's great train shed (c. 1839) has a span of 72 feet. When it was built, it had a wider single span than any existing roof. All the buildings of Bristol Old Station are being restored by the Brunel Engineering Centre Trust.*

8. Clifton

Clifton means 'place of the cliffs', aptly enough, since parts of it teeter at the threshold of the Avon Gorge. But to most Bristolians it means the fashionable upper part of the city, one of the largest areas of Georgian and Regency domestic architecture outside Bath, where neoclassical terraces variegate a lively shopping area replete with wine-bars, delicatessen, antique stores and restaurants. The layout of this former village is haphazard and unpredictable, reflecting erratic bursts of building activity, followed by lulls and slumps and resurgences of confidence and optimism. 'No one can resist the charm of Clifton's confusion', wrote Nikolaus Pevsner, succumbing to it himself. Development at Clifton began around 1775, prompted by the boom of Hotwells Spa (see below), only to stop abruptly during the Napoleonic Wars, when a visitor described the 'melancholy spectacle' of 'the silent and falling houses'. But speculation began afresh during the Regency period, when many of the crescents and squares were erected in the modish Grecian style. A pleasing feature of Clifton is its narrow walled lanes, tree-lined or softened by founts of greenery, that connect the more spacious architectural ensembles: the walker moves from a prospect of cooped-in cosiness to the sudden dramatic panorama of a terrace with sweeping cornices and lacey balconies.

Clifton Down Road is a good point from which to explore both Regency and Victorian aspects of Clifton. Starting just north of the junction with Princess Victoria Street, stroll eastwards down Boyce's Avenue, where there is a group of Georgian buildings (1763) named after the wigmaker–speculator who wished to provide comfortable lodgings for visitors to Hotwells. A small cobbled cul-de-sac leads from the avenue to the Albion, a popular public house. Beyond the Italianate archway lies Victoria Square, a massive conception dominated by the Royal Promenade (c. 1845), its north-west side, designed by John Foster. There is a touch of bombast here in the round-arched windows, rusticated piers and ebullient scrollwork.

The central gardens of the square are bisected by a diagonal path which leads to Clifton Road and the Fosseway. At the angle of these two roads is the entrance to Birdcage Walk. This most refreshing path passes beneath a series of iron hoops intertwined with climbing plants, traverses a large cemetery and comes out at Clifton Hill, the site of the early village, with the big three-storeyed and pilastered Chesterfield Hospital (1742) rising on the right flank and the Bishop's House on the left.

The remnants of the former village green, a bumpy expanse of grass bounded by roads, are prominent from here. To the east is Clifton's most opulent Georgian mansion, Clifton Hill House, built by Isaac Ware in 1747 for Paul Fisher, a wealthy merchant whose monogram is traced out on the pediment. This haughty Palladian gesture now belongs to Bristol University but was once the family home of John Addington Symonds (1840–93), the Victorian poet and essayist who wrote a notable history of the Italian renaissance, a critical work on Shelley, and was himself the subject of a recent fine biographical study by Phyllis Grosskurth. He was always romantically attached to his early home: 'Clifton, now as ever, is full of vague yet powerful associations. When will this Circe cease to brew enchantments for my soul?' Across the way from Clifton Hill House stands the impressive pile of Goldney House (c. 1723), which epitomises the early expansion of Clifton. Unfortunately the house has been much altered but the gardens contain an exuberant structural lark, a wonderful octangular grotto, encrusted with shells, minerals, Bristol diamonds (quartz flakes found in the Avon Gorge) and other shiny petrifactions. There is a sitting lion, a lifelike lioness, and a statue of Neptune holding a vessel out of which water gushes. No wonder visitors to this marvellous place have been inspired to verse. Henry Jones, who came here in the 18th century, described how

> . . . each congenial guest with joy invades
> The fountains, grottos, and the clear cascades . . .

A Gothic tower stores water for the grotto and a crouching Baroque figure of Hercules brandishes his club ominously. Thomas Goldney, the wealthy Quaker merchant who reaped part of his profits from privateering, put great care and energy into the project, filling the gravel walks with orange and lemon trees 'and a small piece of water abounding in gold and silver fish, supplied from a natural fountain'. Goldney House is now a Hall of Residence for the University and there is a self-catering block of students' dwellings which have been designed so as not to obtrude on their romantic setting. The gardens are well worth a visit and they are open to the public at certain specified times under the National Gardens Scheme.

Goldney Lane leads downhill beside the house via Ambra Vale to the area known as Hotwells. It was formerly rather run-down, but now a phoenix-like spirit is apparent, particularly in the number of new apartment blocks which have sprung up at the western end of Hotwell Road. Even the older Georgian and Victorian buildings, set on the higher slopes above the harbour, display a full quota of crisp white window frames and flower tubs at their entrances. Hotwells, of course, is of considerable historical importance as the heart of the spa upon which the early growth of Clifton was founded. Its story conforms to the classic pattern of such ventures – brisk patronage in Georgian times trailing off into near-total neglect by the end of the 18th century. During the 1780s it was among the most visited spas in the kingdom and chosen by Fanny Burney as the setting for her vivacious novel *Evelina* (1778). Like Bath, it had its master of ceremonies and entertained guests with a chamber orchestra, dress balls and public breakfasts. The source of this celebrity was a spring of warm water which bubbled out from the Avon mud below St Vincent's Rocks at a rate of sixty gallons a minute, at a temperature of 76°F, and was sold all over the world. Daniel Defoe visited Bristol in 1724 and counted some fifteen glasshouses engaged in bottling and distribution; the water was later described as 'sparkling and abounding with air bubbles of a whitish colour'. At least one visitor, however, complained that it contained

64 *Erected* c. *1809 in the Mall as the Clifton Assembly Rooms and Hotel, this unusual composition is marked by variety rather than by coherence of classical principles; the oriel windows between the Ionic columns are particularly idiosyncratic.*

river and tidal effluent, which was probably true, as the spring lay some 26 feet below the level of the Avon's high tide. On 1 November 1755 the water turned as red as blood, an occurrence that, according to the record of a certain Captain Manby, sent everyone flying to the churches, 'where prayers were offered to avert the apparent approach of the destruction'. (This curious augury was later attributed to an earthquake in faraway Lisbon.) But when the French war ended, the resorts on the Continent were taken up once more and the spa declined and deteriorated. Its few visitors were chiefly the terminally ill who could not travel abroad; some of them were so sick that they almost died on arrival, and a group of houses near the spa was sinisterly called 'Death Row'.

Dowry Square was Hotwells' chief residential area; the Assembly Rooms, for balls, card-playing and evening parties, were erected near here. Visitors could also enjoy pleasure gardens, a small theatre on Jacob's Wells Road, and a shopping colonnade next to the Pump House. During the spa's declining years Dr Beddoes set up his 'Pneumatic Institution' at No. 6 Dowry Square. He was one of several who believed that cows' breath possessed strong medicinal qualities, helpful for the curing of tuberculosis. It must have been an odd experience being treated by the learned doctor, and waking up each morning with a cow poking its amiable head through the curtains. The Clifton landladies began to complain, stating that 'they had not furnished their rooms for cattle'. Beddoes' assistant during this period was the young Humphry Davy, inventor of the safety lamp, who greatly impressed the poet Coleridge when they met. A plaque refers to his early experiments into the nature of nitrous oxide (laughing gas) which 'led him to suggest a practical means of anaesthesia'. Another physician who worked for Beddoes was the compiler of the famous thesaurus, Dr Roget. Thomas Lovell Beddoes, the author of *Death's Jest Book* – a curiously macabre collection of poems – was the eccentric doctor's brilliant offspring.

From Dowry Square it is an uphill but enjoyable walk to Royal York Crescent. Hopechapel Hill, rising from the square, takes its name from the chapel (now renovated as a community centre) founded by Lady Hope and Lady Glenorchy in 1768. A path to the right, about halfway up the hill, leads to the woody reaches of Glendale. Above rises Cornwallis Crescent, which was begun in 1720; the architect was John Wood the Elder, who inaugurated the great neoclassical building developments at Bath. A detour to the west takes the walker across Granby Hill to Windsor Terrace, set slightly lower down and commanding a breathtaking view of the Cumberland Basin, where the enormous red-brick warehouses – sombre and castle-like with Venetian Gothic embellishments – preside over the River Avon and the flattish area of bypasses and neo-Tudor brick housing estates. The swish and rumble of traffic electrifies the air, even at this considerable height, but this does not distract from the Palladian dignity. In the manner of much of Bath's architecture, the concept is palatial and proud, with the added excitement of a terminal building perched at the cliff edge. The terrace was begun in 1790 and among its famous residents was Hannah More, novelist, playwright, educationalist and philanthropist. She was born in 1745 at Fishponds and her fluent pen brought her a wide public and early acclaim. But her literary impulse was tempered by her passionate commitment to improving the conditions of the poor and fostering Bible-reading. She bustled around the

65 *No. 20 Sion Hill, very spruce, like so many of the sought-after houses in Clifton.*

Somerset countryside, founding Sunday schools, censuring the bibulous revels of the Mendip miners and attracting praise tinged with cynical mockery – 'Holy Hannah' was her nickname. For several years she ran an Academy for Young Ladies in Park Street, and she lived to the age of 88. There are two plaques to her in Bristol, at No. 4 Windsor Terrace and No. 45 Park Street. The end house was the home of William Watts (see p. 78), who invested his fortune in creating the terrace but went bankrupt in 1794; the cost of raising the buttress wall precipitated his financial collapse.

Granby Hill climbs on past Cornwallis Crescent and up to Royal York Gardens. The showpiece hereabouts is Royal York Crescent, perhaps the most impressive of Clifton's terraces, a calm and stately arc of Regency houses begun in 1791 but not completed until 1820 (owing to bankruptcies caused by the French war). The hillside setting is perfect, catching the morning sunshine and affording magnificent views of spires, roofscapes and the distant hill of Dundry. A broad raised pavement flanks the buildings, whose tent-shaped verandahs gracefully drape the sharp symmetry of their windows. Below, big-boughed chestnut trees line Royal York Gardens.

To the south of the western end of the crescent is an extraordinary cul-de-sac called the Paragon (c. 1809–15). This tree-shaded crescent is unusual because it turns its convex and not its concave side to the valley. The convex semicircular entrances served by curved double doors confer an atmosphere of elegant grimness, further heightened by the sombre aspect of the narrow little road with its shaded park. Idiosyncratic and highly effective, the Paragon was designed by John Drew. In 1813 he became bankrupt and the unfinished houses were completed by the builder Stephen Hunter.

Wellington Terrace and Sion Hill (**65**) continue the curve of the Paragon and sweep up to Clifton Suspension Bridge and the Downs. Sion Hill was begun in 1784 and is noted for its bow-fronted Regency dwellings. Opposite the Avon Gorge Hotel, Caledonia Place (**66**) branches off to the right to form the southern block of an elongated square, Georgian in style if not in date. At the eastern end of this is the Mall, an elegant and much-patronised part of Clifton, celebrated for its annual fair, antique dealers and stylish shops and restaurants. Caledonia Place was begun in 1843; the horse-mounting blocks by the road are souvenirs of its more leisured age.

Verandahs and railings enhance some of the buildings in West Mall, the northern block of the 'square', and there are some unusual footscrapers simulating harps and hawks. Lord Macaulay stayed at No. 16 in 1852 – his mother ran a girls' school in Park Street. The Clifton Club in the Mall was originally put up as an Assembly Rooms and hotel in 1809, complete with 'sets of apartments, drawing rooms, a coffee room; a shop for pastry and confectionery with an adjoining room for soups, fruit, and ices; hot, cold and vapour baths'. Francis Howard Greenway, the architect of the Club, moved from Mangotsfield to Bristol in 1805 and set up a successful building business; later he turned to speculation and was arrested for forgery and thrown into Newgate Jail. But his death sentence was commuted and he was deported to Australia; here he prospered again, finally attaining the title 'Father of Australian Architecture'. A plaque on Fairfax House (in Newgate, near Castle Park), the site of the prison, commemorates his incarceration in 1812 and also the death in 1743 of another distinguished inmate, the dissolute but gifted poet Richard Savage.

66 Parts of Caledonia Place were not begun until the 1840s yet they are distinctly Georgian in style. Lush hanging baskets pick this house out from the rest of the terrace. Lord Macaulay stayed at No. 16, next door, in 1852.

The special attractiveness of Clifton is not just its profusion of well-proportioned houses and civilised shopping areas, but its setting for them – 442 acres of countryside, known as the Downs. An Act of Parliament (1861) secured the public ownership of Clifton Down, while Durdham Down was purchased from the Lords of the Manor for £15,000. In medieval times the Downs served for sheep-grazing and in the 18th century they became notorious as the haunt of petty thieves, footpads and underpaid colliers from Kingswood. The miners opposed the turnpiking of the Downs in 1727, and smashed down the tollgates connecting Westbury and Stoke Bishop. Troops were called in to restore order, but the gates were subsequently demolished again, 'by men disguised in women's clothes and wearing high-crowned hats'. The miners were imitating their Welsh brothers, who had formed a group called the Daughters of Rebecca, taking the text from Genesis: 'And they

67 *The north-west front of the Mansion House (1867), adorned with the city coat of arms, has a magnificent view over the Downs.*

68 *The massive piers of Brunel's Clifton Suspension Bridge rise up powerfully against the soft backdrop of Leigh Woods; this view disguises the spectacular span, of 702 feet.*

blessed Rebecca, and said . . . may your descendants possess the gate of those who hate them.' A part of the Downs, now Pembroke Road, was called Gallows' Acre Lane after the gibbet that stood there, and legend has it that ghosts of the executed men, such as Shenkin Protheroe (executed March 1783), stalk though Clifton at night shaking their gallows-chains. They might have difficulty now in identifying some of their old haunts, encroached on by the homes of the well-to-do merchants who acquired their fortunes with more finesse and less audacity.

One of the minor highlights of the Downs – always of great interest to schoolchildren – is the Observatory, which overlooks the Avon Gorge slightly to the north of the suspension bridge. This stubby white building, jauntily crenellated, started out as a snuff mill but was burned down in 1777. William West had it rebuilt as a tower and observatory in 1829 and installed an optical novelty of great charm, the camera obscura. The polished-glass condensing mirror revolves and encompasses the fluttering foliage, ships breasting up the gorge and the casual intimacies of picnickers and strollers on the Downs. From here, there are rock-cut steps leading underground to St Vincent's (or Giant's) Cave, which takes its name from a former Chapel of St Vincent that once occupied the clifftop above but presumably fell into ruin. An ecclesiastical tile and a fragment of a mullion from the chapel or oratory were found

in the cave, which may itself have been used as a place of meditation or prayer. The clergyman and diarist Francis Kilvert provides an account of a visit to Clifton in 1874, when he went down in 'the slush and mire and darkness of the Giant's Cave'.

From the Observatory's stubby knoll there are excellent views down the Avon Gorge, dominated by Isambard Kingdom Brunel's suspension bridge (**2, 68**). This stunning feat of engineering, Bristol's most famous single image, was partly financed by William Vick, a local merchant who died in 1752, leaving a legacy for building a bridge across the gorge. In 1829, when enough money had accumulated, the Merchant Venturers organised a design competition, appointing the elderly Thomas Telford – famous for his Menai Straits suspension bridge – to give the casting vote on the various submissions. He rejected Brunel's tensile, fluent design, offering one of his own instead, a comically cautious conception employing two huge masonry piers rising from the foot of the cliff and supporting the superstructure. This was rejected by the judges and eventually Brunel's blueprint was picked out as the winner. His design, however, was modified during the actual construction, and decorative sphinxes, originally intended to surmount the tall pylons, were omitted. The building of the bridge, a single span of 702 feet, was constantly held up by failing funds and apathy, and was not completed until 1864, some five years after Brunel's death. Pacing the walkway is a most exciting experience and the jagged sublimity of the setting has acted as an incentive to those intent on taking permanent leave of this curious world. One such desolated soul was Sarah Ann Henley, who, in 1885, after a lovers' quarrel,

69, 70 Bristol Zoo, open all year round, is renowned not only for its varied and extensive collection of animals (right, a polar bear) but also for its beautiful gardens.

flung herself over the edge of the railings, but her ballooning petticoats parachuted her to safety, and she lived to be 85. Leigh Woods (NT), a rural escape from the sometimes hectic pace of the city, beckon invitingly from the other side of the Avon Gorge. Deciduous foliage softens the bleak precipice, and the gorge itself is famous for its rare flowers and trees, including a unique species of whitebeam, called *bristoliensis*.

The road called Clifton Down sweeps north past the Observatory and east to the Mansion House (**67**), which overlooks the Downs at the junction with Canynge Road. This is the residence of the Lord Mayor of Bristol and the wall bears the city coat of arms: two unicorns support a crested shield adorned with a merchant ship and castle. The ceremony of tea with the Lady Mayoress on the first Wednesday of every month, from 3 to 5 pm, is an honoured tradition enjoyed by the people of Bristol. The civic plate is highly burnished and there is a 16th-century silver salver which was stolen, sawn into 167 bits, recovered and riveted together again. The Mansion House dates from 1867 when Alderman Proctor employed the architects George and Henry Godwin to erect 'a functional styleless building with large well-built rooms and an internal gallery'. The city inherited it as a Mansion House in 1874; it replaced the one in Queen Square destroyed during the Bristol Riots of 1831. Despite the avowed plainness of its conception, it now typifies the period flavour with its heavy bay windows, ground-floor rustication and air of solidity. As Clare Crick observed in her book on Victorian buildings in Bristol (1975), the gabled Gothic style never properly came to roost in Clifton, which preferred Italianate round-headed windows, quoins and string-courses.

North of the Mansion House, in College Road, a long continuous wall marks the confines of Bristol Zoo. The entrance gate is at the junction of Clifton Down and College Road, facing the open hummocky Downs. The zoo can be considered as the most spectacular example of the early democratisation of the Downs; it dates from 1834 when the Bristol, Clifton and West of England Zoological Society was formed. There are some twelve acres of beautiful gardens (**69**) where the visitor can wander among aviaries and cages, watching penguins waddle and plunge, monkeys cavort in their splendid minareted temple and lions snarl sulkily in their barred cells. The white tigers here are famous (the only ones in Europe) and there is a new purpose-built reptile house (1980) boasting over a hundred snakes and reptiles, which slither and bask luxuriously in their insulated penthouses.

On the other side of Guthrie Road (behind the zoo) is Clifton College (**71**), a famous public school, renowned for character training. It was founded in 1862 and became noted for its enlightened outlook, taking in a number of Jewish boys and developing a strong scientific slant. The first buildings, the Big School, Headmaster's House (in Cecil Road) and Chapel, date from the 1860s and additions were made in Gothic style during the 1920s. The Close is dominated by a statue of Earl Haig (1861–1928), Commander-in-Chief of the British Expeditionary Forces in France and Flanders during the First World War, a former pupil whose attitude to military strategy was satirised by Joan Littlewood in her jaunty extravaganza *O What a Lovely War*. The poet Henry

71 *The first buildings of Clifton College were designed in the mid 19th century by Charles Hansom. The chapel, added 1865–7 as a memorial to Canon Guthrie, the driving force behind the foundation of the college, has been enlarged many times and was refashioned 1909–10; its octagon is based on Ely Cathedral's. Earl Haig, a former pupil, watches over the immaculate playing fields.*

72 *The Roman Catholic Cathedral of SS Peter and Paul (1970–3) is easily recognised by its unusual and daring tripartite concrete spire.*

Newbolt (1862–1938) was another pupil; he cherished an unbounded love for his school. His much-anthologised 'Vitaï Lampada' begins by describing a cricket match as seen from the Clifton Close and then transfers the same breezy determination to 'play the game' to a bloody, bullet-torn desert war. A more recent pupil at the college was John Cleese, pioneer of the new comedy of manic desperation.

South of Clifton College, bounded by Clifton Park and Pembroke Road, the modern Roman Catholic cathedral of SS Peter and Paul, consecrated in 1973, can be picked out by its gaunt reinforced concrete spire (**72**). Percy Thomas Partnership were the architects and their monogram is incised on the building. The design incorporates the liturgical decisions of the Second Vatican Council, enabling the congregation to have a good view of the high altar. An elongated hexagon forms the main worshipping space, and the interior, although sparsely furnished, is highly attractive, with symbolic windows by Henry Haig and a font of Portland and Purbeck stone by Simon Verity. The exterior panels of the building are made of pink Aberdeen granite chips, creating a warm tone that offsets the soaring starkness.

9. Around Bristol

Ashton Court Estate

Only 2 miles from the centre of Bristol, on the western side of the Avon Gorge, Ashton Court Estate comprises over 800 acres of beautiful woods and dales, including what is thought to be the oldest deer park in England. The City of Bristol acquired the immense estate in 1960 and it has become a venue for numerous popular events: the International Balloon Fiesta (**73**) in August, the North Somerset Agricultural Show, the Classic and Historic Motoring Montage and the Bristol Horse Show. There are acres of parkland through which red and fallow deer (reintroduced 1970) roam wild, two approach and putt golf courses, a nature trail and facilities for orienteering. The estate was first enclosed by Thomas de Lyons in 1391; the mansion itself is enormously long, combining Gothic, Jacobean and Tudor work. There are 15th-century

73 *The grounds of Ashton Court and the sky above are filled with colour during the International Balloon Fiesta, held there every August.*

74 *The cottages of Blaise Castle Hamlet (1810–12), varied in detail and ornament, form a pretty ensemble around the ornamental pump.*

windows of heraldic glass and the south-west wing has been attributed to Inigo Jones, who may have been commissioned by the Smyth family, the Elizabethan and Jacobean owners. Thomas Smyth, a Stuart Member of Parliament, lived here with nine maidservants, twenty serving men and a regular supply of comic gags, being one of the last landowners to employ a full-time jester.

Blaise Castle Estate

The Blaise Castle Estate is at Henbury, about 4 miles north-west of the city centre. The castle (1766) is no arrogant medieval stronghold, but a sham, a Gothic frolic built by Thomas Farr within the ramparts of an Iron Age fort. (The name 'Blaise', comes from St Blasius, a patron of wool-gatherers and sympathetic to bonfires.) The famous landscape architect Humphry Repton planned the gardens and the long winding carriage drive (1796) joining Henbury Hill and the new Blaise Castle House (1795–7). This Georgian mansion was designed by William Paty, architect of Royal York Crescent, for J. S. Harford, a Bristol banker, and now houses a branch of the City Museum. Its speciality is agricultural and social history and its varied collection includes dolls, costumes, musical instruments, snuff boxes, constables' truncheons and craft tools. John Nash's conservatory (1806) is a plain but effective design comprising a stone arcade of seven glazed bays. The dairy, also by Nash, now displays the museum's dairying collection. But the main attraction of Blaise must be the grounds, some 400 acres of woodland, lawn,

75 *Arno's Castle, a fantasy constructed from blocks of slag and originally used as stables.*

hillside and running water. In the valley the Hazel Brook flows by Stratford Mill, rebuilt 1954, and there are such delights as the Butcher's Cave, an 18th-century grotto where the big stones resemble joints of meat, and the 'footprints' of the Giant Goram, immortalised in one of Chatterton's Rowley poems.

Finally there is Blaise Castle Hamlet (NT), a totally picturesque estate village (**74**), east of Castle House, designed by John Nash and Humphry Repton's son in 1810–12. Ten thatched cottages with tall pepperpot chimneys cluster around a smooth green and the ornamental pump in the middle. The grouping of the buildings ensures the privacy of each entrance – architectural strategy conniving to stop tenants' idle gossiping.

The Devil's Cathedral

Arno's Vale, about 2 miles from central Bristol on the Bath Road, has a most unusual castle (**75**) composed of oblong blocks of bluish black slag – leftovers from the copper-smelting process. It was built for a rich copper smelter, Mr Reeves, in 1760, and the castle, adorned with crosses, vertical slits, chalky white pinnacles and crenellations, served as stables to his more sedate Gothic mansion up the road. Horace Walpole called it the 'Devil's Cathedral' – a very good description, if one recognises that its 'sinister gaiety' recalls a pantomine devil rather than Satan himself. Not far away is the ornamental gateway and Arno's Court (Mr Reeves' house), now a hotel.

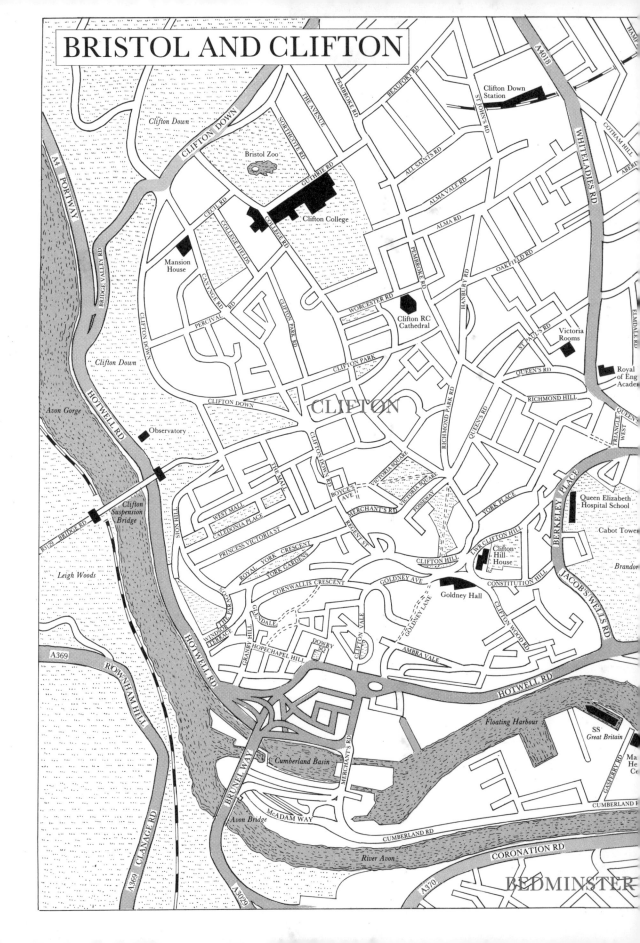

BRISTOL AND CLIFTON